Baki Kasapligil
Mills College, Oakland 13, Calif
U. S. A.

Predmont
June 1966 ———

D0819968

GARDENS OF DELIGHT

Frontispiece :   The Gallant Gardener. Hochst porcelain group. c. 1750.
British Museum.

MILES & JOHN HADFIELD

GARDENS

OF

DELIGHT

LITTLE, BROWN AND COMPANY

Boston   Toronto

Printed in Great Britain

Introduction

Fundamentally, all gardening is the transference of a vision into a touchable and seeable reality. It may be a re-creation on earth of the garden from which man came, or an anticipation of the paradise to which, if he behaves himself, he will eventually journey. It may be an open-air extension of an Italian villa, or a setting (as in the time of Louis XIV) for the incomparable palace of a 'Sun King'; a place of subtle architectural design for processions, masques, and fêtes; a scene for human pomp and circumstance where man with his arts and sciences brazenly defies nature, 'torturing' it—as the school of landscapers used to say—into symmetry, law, and order.

In hot countries, where sun and drought are the enemies of comfort, the dream is of splashing fountains, of cool colonnades, and of avenues or canals shaded by that tree of admirable 'pulchritude and procerity', the *chenar* or oriental plane. Here the objective is voluptuous relaxation. In utter contrast is the garden evolved in China and developed in Japan. This is a place for reflection, a small cosmos representing, but not imitative of, the more significant features of the natural world. The whole is a well-understood symbol or series of symbols, such as we find in Chinese and Japanese art. In both these countries horticulture and the selection and breeding of plants to conform to certain ideals were practised centuries before they were in the western world.

Quite distinct was the vision that the English philosophers, poets, essayists, and painters saw for the first time in the early eighteenth century, and which led to the so-called 'landscape' and 'picturesque' gardens. The fashion spread to France, as *le jardin anglais*, and subsequently far beyond; it is the basis of most modern free landscaping. True, Nature had little enough to do with the movement, which was first concerned with the introduction of irregularity, asymmetry, and the replacement of straight lines by serpentines.

A major inspiration was the view of the Roman *campagna* as seen in the seventeenth-century paintings of Claude and Poussin. The resultant landscape garden (created in the moist English climate!) was full of classical and literary allusions. One of the first examples, William Kent's Rousham in Oxfordshire, was praised by Horace Walpole for being 'a Daphne in little; the sweetest little groves, streams, glades, porticoes, cascades and river, imaginable; all the scenes are perfectly classic'. Here, indeed, was no more than a new kind of artifice, a strangely unnatural view of nature and unclassical view of the classic—from which the formal garden of Le Nôtre was the true and direct descendant.

But let us not criticize; gardening is fortunately not rational, and the ideas of Lord Shaftesbury, Burke, Addison, Pope, Walpole, and Shenstone provided a new kind of delight, new elysiums where the ancient gods (in some instances) still dwell, and pastoral arcadies which now provide delightful sites for the picnicking motorist.

Our book, also, is not wholly rational. We have tried to reflect some of the delights of gardens as recorded and illuminated by poets and philosophers, essayists, diarists, and travellers, and as illustrated by painters and potters, draughtsmen and sculptors. The richness of the material available, however, and the vastness of the subject, have imposed a severe selectivity. How to select? We have attempted to provide a balanced composition, but we admit to having been influenced by two dominant considerations: first, our own personal predilections (and as every garden is, or should be, a personal creation, we make no apologies for this); secondly, an inclination to avoid the familiar, the conventional, or the hackneyed, unless it positively demands inclusion.

On the assumption that the reader is in the same fortunate position as Nicholas Bacon of Gillingham, Esquire, to whom, in 1658, Sir Thomas Browne dedicated his learned study of the Garden of Cyrus, and that 'you have wisely ordered your vegetable delights beyond the reach of exception', we would like to express Sir Thomas's hope:

> *that in this Garden Discourse, we range into extraneous things, and many parts of Art and Nature; we follow herein the examples of old and new Plantations, wherein noble spirits contented not themselves with Trees, but by the attendance of Aviaries, Fish-Ponds, and all variety of Animals, they made their gardens the Epitome of the earth.*

Contents

Acknowledgements

The authors are indebted to the under-mentioned for permission to quote extracts from copyright sources:

Earl De La Warr ('The Apple' by Lady Margaret Sackville); Allen & Unwin Ltd ('The Lychee Tree' from *The Temple*: trs. Arthur Waley); American Philosophical Society (*Thomas Jefferson's Garden Book*); estate of the late Gerald Bullett ('Gardeners' and 'The Garden at Night' from *Poems*); Clarendon Press (Essay on Persian Gardens by V. Sackville-West from *The Legacy of Persia*, ed. A. J. Arberry); Constable & Co Ltd and Alfred Knopf Inc ('Alarm at first entering the Yangtze Gorges' and 'Planting Flowers on the Eastern Embankment' from *170 Chinese Poems*: trs Arthur Waley); Curtis Brown Ltd and Doubleday & Co Inc ('Honour the Gardener' from *The Garden*: V. Sackville-West—copyright 1946 by V. Sackville-West); J. M. Dent & Sons Ltd and Macmillan Co, New York (*Two Acres and a Mill*: R. Gathorne-Hardy); G. Duckworth & Co Ltd (*On the Making of Gardens*: Sir George Sitwell); Faber & Faber Ltd (*The Curious Gardener*: Jason Hill); Wm Heinemann Ltd and the estate of Edith Wharton (*The Secret Garden*: F. Hodgson Burnett); David Higham Associates Ltd and Duckworth & Co Ltd ('The Gardener' from *Collected Poems*: Sacheverell Sitwell); David Higham Associates, Macmillan & Co Ltd and Vanguard Press Inc (Edith Sitwell's 'The Strawberry' from *The Canticle of the Rose* (Macmillan), *The Collected Poems of Edith Sitwell* (Vanguard)—copyright 1954 by Dame Edith Sitwell); Hodder & Stoughton Ltd and Doubleday & Co Inc (*The Story of my Life*: Helen Keller); Mrs Essex Hope, Jonathan Cape Ltd and Macmillan Co, New York (*Kilvert's Diary*: Francis Kilvert); Lee & Pembertons (*Home and Garden*: Gertrude Jekyll); Percy Lubbock and Jonathan Cape Ltd (*Earlham*); Macmillan & Co Ltd and Viking Press (*Episode of Sparrows*: Rumer Godden); Mrs Mewton-Wood ('Magic'; W. J. Turner); Laurence Pollinger Ltd and Wm Heinemann Ltd ('Allotments' from Richard Church's *Collected Poems*); L. Pollinger Ltd, Wm Heinemann Ltd, Viking Press Inc and the estate of the late Mrs Frieda Lawrence ('Bavarian Gentians' from *The Complete Poems of D. H. Lawrence*); L. Pollinger Ltd, André Deutsch Ltd and Wm Morrow & Co Inc ('Apples' from *My Many-coated Man*: Laurie Lee); L. Pollinger Ltd and the estate of Ray L. Murphy (*Edward Lear's Indian Journal*); L. Pollinger Ltd, Jonathan Cape Ltd and Holt, Rinehart & Winston Inc ('After Apple Picking' and 'The Rose Family' from *Complete Poems of Robert Frost*—copyright 1928, 1930, 1939 by Holt, Rinehart & Winston Inc, copyright renewed © 1956, 1958 by Robert Frost); L. Pollinger Ltd and the estate of Edith Wharton (*Italian Villas and their Gardens*: Edith Wharton); Routledge & Kegan Paul Ltd (*Diary of a Scotch Gardener*: T. Blaikie); Martin Secker & Warburg Ltd (*Fountains in the Sand*: Norman Douglas); Mrs Helen Thomas ('Digging' by Edward Thomas); Mrs C. M. Villiers-Stuart and B. T. Batsford Ltd (*Spanish Gardens*); and Miss E. A. Wolfe ('The Tulip' from *Kensington Gardens*: Humbert Wolfe).

List of Illustrations

LIST OF ILLUSTRATIONS

LIST OF ILLUSTRATIONS

LIST OF ILLUSTRATIONS

◆◇◆

1

The Fabulous and the Ideal

How little we are told of that first garden of all, 'east-ward in Eden'. We know more of the land of Havilah with its gold, bdellium, and onyx stone than of that place 'where the man was put to work and dress every tree that was pleasant to the sight and good for food'. This lack of information has fortunately allowed the poets freedom to interpret Eden in the idiom of their time. Joshua Sylvester translated du Bartas's sixteenth-century account thus:

Heer, underneath a fragrant hedge reposes,
Full of all kinds of sweet all-coloured Roses,
Which (one would think) the angels daily dresse
In true love-knots, tri-angles, lozenges.
   Anon he walketh in a levell lane,
On eyther side beset with shady Plane,
Whose archèd boughs, for Frize and Cornich bear
Thick groves, to change from future change of air:
Then in a path impal'd, in pleasant wise,
With sharp-sweet Orange, Limon, Citron trees;
Whose leavie twigs, that intricately tangle,
Seem painted walls, whereon true fruits do dangle.
   Now in a plenteous orchard planted rare
With un-graft trees, in checker, round and square:
Whose goodly fruits so on his will do wait,
That plucking one, another's ready straight:
And having tasted all (with due satiety)
Finds all one goodness, but in taste variety.

Du Bartas—or his translator—was clearly influenced by the formality of the enclosed garden of his time. Oddly enough, the painters of the fifteenth and sixteenth centuries tended to a less formal, more 'pictur-

esque' treatment of their garden backgrounds when depicting Adam and
Eve. One of the most vivid treatments of this theme is that in the left
wing of Hugo van der Goes's diptych of the Temptation and the Fall,
now in the Kunsthistorisches Museum, Vienna. Apart from the engagingly fanciful treatment of the human serpent, this picture is notable for
the brilliant realism of its flower painting. The place traditionally taken
by fig leaves is here occupied by an iris, a flower whose ancient symbolism
we shall discuss later. Hugo van der Goes (who died in 1482) was not
one of the famous specialist flower painters of the Low Countries, but his
great Portinari altarpiece, in the Uffizi in Florence, contains exquisite
details of flowers in vases, including white and blue iris, and shows that
he possessed as keen a botanical sense as any of the later Dutch or Flemish masters.

As du Bartas's description of Eden proceeds he becomes more fanciful:

> Anon he stalketh with an easy stride,
> By some clear river's lilly-pavèd side,
> Whose sand's pure gold, whose pebbles precious gemms,
> And liquid silver all the curling streams:
> Whose chiding murmur, mazing in and out,
> With crystall cisterns moats a mead about:
> And th'artless bridges, over-thwart this torrent,
> Are rocks self-archèd by the eating current:
> Or loving Palms, whose lusty females (willing
> Their marrow boyling loves to be fulfilling
> And reach their husband-trees on th'other banks)
> Bow their stiffe backs, and serve for passing planks.

Hugo van der Goes evidently did not regard the river as an essential
element in his Eden, but it is to be seen in the background of many other
treatments of the theme, most notably in a painting attributed to Jan van
Scorel, now at Temple Newsam, Leeds, of which another version is in
the Metropolitan Museum in New York. Van Scorel's 'curling streams'
wind their way elaborately between forests into a far, far distance.

Animals appear in great variety and, of course, in perfect amity in
many paintings of the Garden of Eden. In the Mauritshuis at The Hague

Hugo van der Goes. The Temptation. c. 1470.
Vienna, Kunsthistorisches Museum.

André Bauchant. Adam and Eve. 1938. *London, Private Collection.*

there is a painting which packs in more than sixty different creatures, including a horse, a peacock, an ostrich, a guinea-pig, various parrots and cockatoos, a lion, a tiger, a panther, domestic poultry, and several fishes. In such a gathering, inevitably, the serpent takes a back seat—in this instance, twining inconspicuously round a bough of the fateful tree. It is hardly surprising that this picture engaged the energies of two painters: Rubens, who painted Adam and Eve, and Jan Breughel, who painted the menagerie.

It is curious to find a somewhat similar, if not so congested, animal crowd scene in a painting by an artist of our own times, André Bauchant (1873–1958). The special interest of this delightful exercise in the *naïf*, however, is the clothing of Adam and Eve in garlands of flowers. This is indeed a true gardener's interpretation, since André Bauchant, who painted the picture in 1938, was for many years a mere 'Sunday painter'; on the other days of the week he worked as a market gardener.

Where *was* Eden? Loudon summed up its situation with his usual thoroughness more than a century ago in his great *Encyclopaedia of Gardening*:

> It was supposed by some to have been situated in Persia; by others in Armenia; and by others in Chaldea, on the north side of the Persian Gulf, near the present Bassora, the river Euphrates dividing there into four streams, in the manner mentioned in Holy Writ. Buckingham tells us that the people of Damascus believe implicitly that the site of Paradise was at El Mezey near that city, now a favourite place of recreation for the Turks. The waters of the Tege and Barrady, which supply the numerous fountains of Damascus, divide there into four streams, and these they suppose to be the four rivers of Moses.
>
> The inhabitants of Ceylon say that Paradise was placed in their country, and they still point out Adam's bridge and Abel's tomb. Sir Alexander Johnston informs us that they also point out as the tree which bore the forbidden fruit, the *Divi Ladner*, or *Tabernaemontana alternifolia* of botanists. In confirmation of this tradition, they refer to the beauty of the fruit, and the fine scent of the flowers, both of which are most tempting. The shape of the fruit gives the idea of a piece having been bitten off; and the inhabitants say it was excellent before Eve ate of it, though it is now poisonous.

Many other fanciful opinions have been given respecting the site of Paradise, and a Swedish professor in the seventeenth century wrote a book to prove it was in Sweden.

To delve deeply into the histories and theories of these various gardens of legend would be a protracted and confusing task. In the rich seventeenth-century prose of his great essay 'Upon the Gardens of Epicurus' Sir William Temple summarized some of them thus:

If we believe the Scripture, we must allow that God Almighty esteemed the life of a man in a garden the happiest He could give him, or else He would not have placed Adam in that of Eden; that it was the state of innocence and pleasure; and that the life of husbandry and cities came after the Fall, with guilt and with labour. Where Paradise was, has been much debated, and little agreed. . . . A Paradise . . . seems to have been a large space of ground, adorned and beautified with all sorts of trees, both of fruits and of forest, either found there before it was inclosed, or planted after; either cultivated like gardens, for shades and for walks, with fountains or streams, and all sorts of plants usual in the climate, and pleasant to the eye, the smell or the taste; or else employed, like our parks, for inclosure and harbour of all sorts of wild beasts, as well as for the pleasure of riding and walking; and so they were of more or less extent, and of differing entertainment, according to the several humours of the Princes that ordered and inclosed them. Semiramis is the first we are told of in story, that brought them in use through her empire, and was so fond of them, as to make one wherever she built, and in all, or most of the provinces she subdued; which are said to have been from Babylon as far as India. The Assyrian kings continued this custom and care, or rather this pleasure, till one of them brought in the use of smaller and more regular gardens: for having married a wife he was fond of, out of one of the provinces, where such paradises or gardens were much in use, and the country lady not well bearing the air or inclosure of the palace in Babylon to which the Assyrian kings used to confine themselves; he made her gardens, not only within the palaces, but upon terraces raised with earth, over the arched roofs, and even upon the top of the highest tower, planted them with all sorts of fruit-trees, as well as other plants and flowers, the most pleasant of that country; and thereby made at least the most airy gardens, as well as the most costly, that have been heard of in the world. . . .

The next gardens we read of, are those of Solomon, planted with all sorts of fruit-trees, and watered with fountains; and though we have no more particular description of them, yet we may find, they were the places where he passed the times of his leisure and delight, where the houses as well as grounds were adorned with all that could be of pleasing and elegant, and were the retreats and entertainments of those among his wives that he loved the best; and 'tis not improbable, that the paradises mentioned by Strabo were planted by this great and wisest King. But the idea of the garden must be very great, if it answers at all to that of the gardener, who must have employed a great deal of his care and of his study, as well as of his leisure and thought, in these entertainments, since he writ of all plants, from the cedar to the shrub.

After Eden, probably the most famous of mythical gardens was that of the Hesperides. Along with the Pleiades and Hyades, these nymphs were the daughters of Atlas. Their names were Hesperis, Aegle (well known to gardeners as a shrub whose vicious spines guard golden but worthless fruits), and Erytheia.

Hera, their mother, was at her nuptials presented with an apple-tree bearing fruit of particular perfection, and this she planted in her own divine garden to be watched over by her three daughters. Where this garden, known by the name of the daughters rather than its owner, was placed has been, as we shall later see, the subject of conjecture. Only one thing seems certain: it was at the spot where the chariot horses of the sun wearily completed their daily journey.

No psychologist—so far as we know—has studied the effects, which seem remarkably consistent, of choice apples upon women. There was no exception in the case of the Hesperides, and in due course their mother found them pilfering and, we must assume, consuming the forbidden fruit. So she obtained the services of the ever-sleepless, hundred-headed dragon Ladon to guard the fruit.

Atlas, it should be mentioned, though not the owner of the apple tree, took a great pride in its cultivation and indeed in the whole of the garden (he had not then assumed the burden that later bowed him down).

The confusion about the situation of the garden goes back to the days of Heracles, who, for his eleventh labour, was commanded to take the golden apples from under the hundred noses of Ladon. We read that he had no idea even of the direction in which the garden lay, but eventually succeeded in his task thanks to a shady trick he played on the gardener Atlas.

'What the gardens of the Hesperides were,' wrote Sir William Temple, 'we have little or no account, further than the mention of them, and thereby the testimony of their having been in use and request, in such remoteness of place, and ambiguity of time.' A solution to this mystery however, was advanced by two archaeologists, the brothers Beechey, who in 1828 published their *Proceedings of the Expedition to Explore the Northern Coast of Africa*:

> Some very singular pits or chasms of natural formation are found in the neighbourhood of Bengazi; they consist of a level surface of excellent soil, of several hundred feet in extent, enclosed within steep, and, for the most part, perpendicular sides of solid rock, rising sometimes to a height of sixty or seventy feet, or more, before they reach the level of the plain in which they are situated. The soil at the bottom of these chasms appears to have been washed down from the plain above by the heavy winter rains, and is frequently cultivated by the Arabs; so that a person, in walking over the country where they exist, comes suddenly upon a beautiful orchard or garden, blooming in secret, and in the greatest luxuriance, at a considerable depth beneath his feet, and defended on all sides by solid walls of rock, so as to be at first sight apparently inaccessible. The effect of these little secluded plots, protected, as it were, from the intrusion of mankind by the steepness and the depth of the barriers which enclose them, is singular and pleasing in the extreme. It was impossible to walk round the edge of these precipices, looking everywhere for some part less abrupt than the rest, by which we might descend into the gardens beneath, without calling to mind the description given by Scylax of the far-famed garden of the Hesperides. This celebrated retreat is stated by Scylax to have been an enclosed spot of about one-fifth of a British mile across, each way, filled with thickly planted fruit trees of various kinds, and inaccessible on all sides. It was situated (on the authority of the same author) at 620 stadia (or fifty geographical miles) from the Port of Barce; and this distance agrees precisely with that of the places here

alluded to from Ptolemeta, the port intended by Scylax. . . . The testimony of Pliny is also very decided in fixing the site of the Hesperides in the neighbourhood of Berenice.

Homer gives us descriptions of two more gardens in the lively world of Greek myth. That of Alcinous was of some four acres in extent and devoted mainly to the cultivation of fruits, vines, and herbs:

> Fenc'd with a green enclosure all around
> Tall thriving trees confess'd the fruitful mold;
> The red'ning apple ripens here to gold,
> Here the blue fig with luscious juice o'erflows,
> With deeper red the full pomegranate glows,
> The branch here bends beneath the weighty pear,
> And verdant olives flourish round the year . . .

In the days when it was believed that the *Odyssey* was history, and not romance written by a woman, this was regarded as giving us the first written record of a hedge.

The other Homeric garden is that of Laertes, of about the same size and style. He was working in it when Ulysses returned from his wanderings.

The origin and details of the hanging gardens of Babylon, surely the most popularly famous of all ancient gardens, were described with much precision (though no one knows with what degree of accuracy) by Diodorus Siculus, who wrote during the decades just before the birth of Christ.

He records that they were built by Cyrus for the sake of a courtesan, who, being Persian by birth and so having a liking for meadows on mountain tops, desired the king to make an artificial plantation to remind her of home. The garden Cyrus made was four hundred feet square. The 'mountain top' on which it was placed was supported by a series of arches built one above another. The highest arch, on which the platform of the garden was laid, was fifty cubits high. The walls were very strong and built at great expense. They were twenty-two feet thick and the openings in them ten feet wide. This huge erection was covered with great beams on which were laid stones sixteen feet long by four feet wide.

These were in turn covered with reeds saturated in bitumen, a layer of tiles and finally sheets of lead—all so that the water would not seep through from earth then piled on so deeply that large trees could thrive in it. The rooms below were stately and used for many purposes, but one contained engines which, through pipes concealed from spectators, drew water up from the Euphrates.

Whether the lady was satisfied by this expansive and expensive scheme is, apparently, not known.

J. C. Loudon's 'esteemed friend', the painter John Martin, 'in his inspired pictures . . . realised all that the vivid and most fertile imagination could conceive of eastern splendour' of this garden. Loudon in his *Encyclopaedia* was able to use engravings of Martin's pictures to illustrate not only Babylon but the gardens of Nineveh. May it not be possible that the learned Loudon was consulted about horticultural matters in these two masterpieces of the art of destruction?

The connexion of Nebuchadnezzar with the gardens was given by Sir Thomas Browne:

> The account of the Pensil or hanging gardens of Babylon, if made by Semiramis, the third or fourth from Nimrod, is of no slender antiquity; which being not framed upon ordinary level ground, but raised upon pillars admitting under-passages, we cannot accept as the first Babylonian Gardens: but a more eminent progress and advancement in that art, than any that went before it; Somewhat answering or hinting the old Opinion concerning Paradise itself, with many conceptions elevated above the plane of the Earth.
>
> Nebuchodonosor, whom some will have to be the famous Syrian King of Diodorus, beautifully repaired that city, and so magnificently built his hanging gardens, that from succeeding writers he had the honour of the first. From whence over-looking Babylon, and all the Region about it, he found no circumscription to the eye of his ambition, till over-delighted with the bravery of this Paradise; in his melancholy metamorphosis he found the folly of that delight, and a proper punishment in the contrary habitation, in wilde plantations and wandrings of the fields.
>
> The Persian Gallants, who destroyed this Monarchy, maintained their Botanicall bravery.

John Martin. The Fall of Babylon. 1819. Mezzotint. *British Museum.*

Persian Miniature. Prince Humay and Princess Humayun in a Garden. 1396.
Paris, Musée des Arts Decoratifs.

The tradition of Persia with its 'Botanicall bravery' has for centuries been one of a country of gardens and flowers in the fertile places among the bleak mountains. Does it not give its name to the most perfect of fruits, the peach, *Prunus persica*? Persian roses are equally famous, and the older books gave the source of such famous garden plants as jasmine and the crown imperial as Persia. Some of these plants, it is now believed, came from much farther afield—the peach probably from the remote mountains of western China—but there is no doubt that to Persia man brought them, and there they were long cultivated before moving further westward. The art of Persia is full of flowers, and by chance it was the little, rare, and exquisite, truly Persian iris that was chosen for the first plate in Curtis's *Botanical Magazine* of 1787.

The word 'paradise' is one of the very few English words taken from the Persian language, deriving from *Pairidaeza*. This is evolved from *pairi*, 'around' and *diz*, 'to form or mould', and the word meant an enclosure or park. It found its way into Europe through Xenophon's *Oeconomicus*, in which he describes how Cyrus himself conducted Lysander round his paradise at Sardis.

There are some glancing references to gardens in Persian legends, and there are many lovely glimpses of them in the miniature paintings which illustrate Persian manuscripts. One of the loveliest, now to be seen in the Musée des Arts Decoratifs in Paris, is an illustration of the story of the Persian Prince Humay and Humayun, daughter of the Khaqan of China. Prince Humay went to seek Humayun in the Far East, having fallen in love with her beauty in a dream. This miniature, which was painted in 1396, shows their first meeting, in dreamlike surroundings whose floral beauty—to occidental eyes at least—surpasses that of the Princess herself.

Pliny described the formal and unchanging design of Persian gardens, with their canals, avenues of plane-trees, buildings, and fountains, upwards of two thousand years ago. Yet, perhaps because of this great reputation, travellers from Europe have for the last few centuries mostly been a little patronizing about the Persians and their gardens. Probably the reason is that their whole outlook is so distinct from the European that unconsciously comparisons were made to the Persians' disadvantage.

An early example of this outlook was Sir James Chardin in 1686. After describing the great wealth of flowers in the Persian spring, he goes on:

> Their roses are white, yellow and red, and others white on one side, yellow on the other; but notwithstanding all this great variety of beautiful flowers, their gardens are not comparable with those of Europe. As flowers are so common they are very little regarded; you see them intermixed with fruit trees and rose bushes without any order; but large walks planted with trees, fountains, cascades, and pleasure houses, at proper distances, are all that must be expected in their finest gardens.
>
> Nor do the Persians take any manner of pleasure in walking in them, any more than in the fields, but set themselves down in some alcove or summer house as soon as they come into them, totally negligent of that exquisite variety that every foreigner is charmed with.

After this disillusioning comment how reassuring it is to consider the reaction of the Spanish conquistadors to the fabulous gardens which they discovered five hundred years ago on the other side of the world, in Mexico. 'Stout Cortez' himself was amazed at what he saw of this ancient civilization in its full majesty. There is no need to speculate on the nature of the gardens, since Prescott's account, based on records, is for all to read:

> Leaving the main land, the Spaniards came on the great dike or causeway, which stretches some four or five miles in length, and divides lake Chalco from Xochicalo in the west. . . .
>
> As they passed along, they beheld the gay spectacle of multitudes of Indians darting up and down in their light pirogues, eager to catch a glimpse of the strangers, or bearing the products of the country to the neighbouring cities. They were amazed also, by the sight of the *chinampas*, or floating gardens—those wandering islands of verdure . . . teeming with flowers and vegetables, and moving like rafts over the waters. . . .
>
> The pride of Iztapalapan, on which its lord had freely lavished his care and his revenues, was its celebrated gardens. They covered an immense tract of land; were laid out in regular squares, and the paths intersecting them were bordered with trellises, supporting

creepers and aromatic shrubs, that loaded the air with perfumes.

The gardens were stocked with fruit trees, imported from distant places, and with the gaudy family of flowers which belong to the Mexican Flora, scientifically arranged, and growing luxuriant in the equable temperature of the table-land. The natural dryness of the atmosphere was counteracted by means of aqueducts and canals that carried water into all parts of the grounds.

In one quarter was an aviary, filled with numerous kinds of birds, remarkable in this region both for brilliancy of plumage and of song. The gardens were intersected by a canal communicating with the Lake of Tezcuco, and of sufficient size for barges to enter from the latter. But the most elaborate piece of work was a huge reservoir of stone, filled to a considerable height with water, well supplied with different sorts of fish. This basin was sixteen hundred paces in circumference, and was surrounded by a walk, made also of stone, wide enough for four persons to go abreast. The sides were curiously sculptured and a flight of steps led to the water below, which fed the aqueducts above noticed, or, collected into fountains, diffused a perpetual moisture.

Such are the accounts transmitted of these celebrated gardens, at a period when similar horticultural establishments were unknown in Europe; and we might well doubt their existence in this semi-civilized land, were it not a matter of such notoricty at the time, and so explicitly attested by the invaders.

But a generation had scarcely passed, after the Conquest, before a sad change came over these scenes so beautiful. The town itself was deserted, and the shore of the lake was strewed with the wreck of buildings which once were its ornament and its glory. The gardens shared the fate of the city. The retreating waters withdrew the means of nourishment, converting the flourishing plains into a foul and unsightly morass, the haunt of loathsome reptiles; and the water-fowl built her nest in what had once been the palaces of princes.

It is only a short step from the Fabulous to the Fantastic, and about half-way we encounter the gothick imagination of that pioneer of the tale of horror, William Beckford, himself a great maker of gardens as well as a builder of follies. His novel *Vathek, An Arabian Tale* (1786), conducts its megalomaniac hero, ninth caliph of the race of the Abassides, and grandson of Haroun al Raschid, to a high mountain near Samarah, whose sides were swarded with wild thyme and basil, and its summit overspread with so delightful a plain, that it might have been taken for the Paradise destined for the faithful. Upon it, grew a hundred thickets of eglantine and other fragrant shrubs; a hundred arbours of roses, entwined with jessamine and honeysuckle; as many clumps of orange trees, cedar and citron; whose branches, interwoven with the palm, the pomegranate, and the vine, presented every luxury that could regale the eye or the taste. The ground was strewed with violets, harebells and pansies; in the midst of which sprung forth tufts of jonquils, hyacinths, and carnations; with every other perfume that impregnates the air. Four Fountains, not less clear than deep, and so abundant as to slake the thirst of ten armies, seemed purposely placed here, to make the scene more resemble the garden of Eden; which was watered by the four sacred rivers.

Here, the nightingale sang the birth of the rose, her well-beloved, and, at the same time, lamented its short-lived beauty; whilst the turtle deplored the loss of more substantial pleasures; and the wakeful lark hailed the rising light, that re-animates the whole creation. Here, more than anywhere, the mingled melodies of birds expressed the various passions they inspired; as if the exquisite fruits which they pecked at pleasure had given them a double energy.

That other early practitioner of the horror story, Mrs Ann Radcliffe, is, surprisingly, rather more restrained in her horticultural *mise-en-scène*.

'On the pleasant banks of the Garonne, in the province of Gascony, stood in the year 1584 the chateau of Monsieur St Aubert.' Thus opens Mrs Radcliffe's three-volume story of *The Mysteries of Udolpho* (1794). The beginning is calm enough; at that time the building was a mere summer cottage. Emily, the heroine, exercised the elegant arts in a long-windowed room which 'opening on the little lawn that surrounded the house, the eye was led between groves of almond, palm-trees, flowering-ash, and myrtle, to the distant landscape, where the Garonne wandered'. Around the chateau

St Aubert had made very tasteful improvements; yet such was his attachment to objects he had remembered from his boyish days, that he had in some instances sacrificed taste to sentiment. There were two old larches that shaded the building, and interrupted the prospect: St Aubert had sometimes declared that he believed he should have been weak enough to have wept at their fall.

In addition to these larches he planted a little grove of beech, pine, and mountain-ash. On a lofty terrace, formed by the swelling bank of the river, rose a plantation of orange, lemon, and palm trees, whose fruit in the coolness of the evening breathed delicious fragrance. With these were mingled a few trees of other species. Here, under the ample shade of a plane-tree that spread its majestic canopy towards the river, St Aubert loved to sit in the fine evenings of summer. . . .

It was a garden poor Emily was often to recall during the harrowing events of the three volumes that follow. And if one reads an old copy one can be pretty sure that someone will have noted in pencil the frequent botanical and horticultural anachronisms!

Young Benjamin Disraeli set much of *Henrietta Temple* (published in the year Queen Victoria came to the throne) in the garden of Armine Place. His description certainly has a fabulous air:

It seemed like a forest in a beautiful romance; a green and bowery wilderness where Boccaccio would have loved to woo and Watteau to paint. So artfully had the walks been planned, that they seemed interminable, nor was there a single point in the whole pleasaunce where the keenest eye could have detected a limit. Sometimes you wandered in those arched and winding walks dear to pensive spirits; sometimes you emerged on a spot of turf blazing in the sunshine, a small and bright savannah, and gazed with wonder on the group of black and mighty cedars that rose from its centre, with their sharp and spreading foliage. The beautiful and the vast blended together; and the moment after you had beheld with delight a bed of geraniums or of myrtles, you found yourself in an amphitheatre of Italian pines.

A strange exotic perfume filled the air: you trod on the flowers of other lands; and shrubs and plants, that usually are only trusted from their conservatories, like sultanas from their jalousies, to sniff the air and recall their bloom, here learning from hardship the philosophy of endurance, had struggled successfully even against northern winters, and wantoned now in native and unpruned luxuriance.

Or again at Ducie Bower in the same novel—and here we see the beginnings of the nineteenth-century love of over-elaboration:

> They stepped into a Paradise, where the sweetest flowers seemed grouped in every combination of the choicest forms; baskets, and vases, and beds of infinite fancy. A thousand bees and butterflies filled the air with their glancing shapes and cheerful music, and the birds from the neighbouring groves joined in the chorus of melody. The wood walks through which they now rambled admitted at intervals glimpses of the ornate landscape, and occasionally the view extended beyond the enclosed limits, and exhibited the clustering and embossed roofs of the neighbouring village, or some woody hill studded with a farmhouse, or a distant spire.

After these journeys of the imagination it is reassuring to turn back and set foot on the solid ground of Jane Austen's England:

> Cleveland was a spacious, modern-built house, situated on a sloping lawn. It had no park, but the pleasure-grounds were tolerably extensive; and, like every other place of the same degree of importance, it had its open shrubbery, and closer wood walk; a road of smooth gravel, winding round a plantation, led to the front; the lawn was dotted over with timber; the house itself was under the guardianship of the fir, the mountain ash, and the acacia, and a thick screen of them all together, interspersed with tall Lombardy poplars, shut out the offices.

'The pleasure-grounds were tolerably extensive', and the Lombardy poplars 'shut out the offices'. That was the rational, well-ordered world of *Sense and Sensibility* in the closing years of the eighteenth century. Miss Austen's description, as always, is deliciously matter-of-fact. Let us now resume the quest of the ideal, the garden that exists only in imagination—or, even more vividly, in recollections of childhood.

Childhood gardens have a perfection never realized in adult life. It is revealing to read a reminiscence of childhood by Samuel Reynolds Hole, who became Dean of Rochester and a learned authority on the culture of the rose. Looking back at the first garden he and his sisters made, at Caunton Manor near Newark, in the eighteen-twenties, he wrote:

The doll's house (the door of which occupied the whole frontage, the architect having forgotten the stairs) stood centrally at the upper end of our domain, representing the family mansion; 'the gardener', a tin soldier in full uniform with fixed bayonet, spent most of his time lying on his stomach, his form being fragile and the situation windy; and the fishponds were triumphs of engineering skill. Mine was a metal pan, which had formerly been used for culinary purposes, placed in an excavation prepared for it, and containing a real fish, about the size of a whitebait, and caught by hand in the brook hard by. One of my sisters produced, I must confess, a more brilliant effect with some bits of looking-glass, but they lacked the gracefulness of nature and the charm of reality.

The grotto, an oyster-barrel placed on its side, and tastefully ornamented with broken pieces of ivy and other evergreens, contained the wives of Noah, Shem, Ham, and Japhet, taken from our ark, and attended by a dog, a cat, and a parrot. They remained in a perpendicular position night and day, and had a fine effect. . . .

The conservatory was a noble construction adjoining the family mansion, but of larger dimensions—a square hand-glass, which looked as though it had been in a phenomenal hail-storm, and had only one qualification for plant culture, a free circulation of air.

I dwell upon these adjuncts to horticulture rather than upon the produce of the soil, because in the latter department we did not attain a like success. We were not on the best of terms with our gardener—the real gardener, not the tin soldier—and he would not help us. Our ways (over the flower-beds) were not his ways, and he objected to the promiscuous use of his syringe and the premature removal of his fruit. We differed, again, on the subject of transplanting. It seemed to us an easier and more satisfactory process to transfer specimens in full beauty from his garden to our own, rather than to watch their tardy growth and tedious efflorescence. Unhappily for us, the specimens did not seem to like it.

Towards the end of the eighteenth century, perhaps as a reflection of the prevailing fashion amongst the ladies at the court of Marie Antoinette for dressing up as milkmaids, there was in England a vogue for painting portraits of well-bred children in the guise of gardeners. In the Mellon Collection there is an enchanting portrait, by Joseph Wright of Derby, of the youthful Sir William Clayton, elegantly clad in silk shirt with frilled collar and puff sleeves, satin waistcoat and buckled shoes, unconvincingly wielding a spade. Equally enchanting—and equally unreal—is a 'fancy painting' by the American John Copley of a young lady gardener whose tiny barrow-load of flowers contrasts amusingly with her enormous black hat.

In this same vein of sophisticated sentiment is a lyric by Thomas Moore, published in *The Casket* in 1835:

> I have a garden of my own,
>   Shining with flowers of every hue;
> I loved it dearly while alone,
>   But I shall love it more with you:
> And there the golden bees shall come,
>   In summer time at break of morn,
> And wake us with their busy hum
>   Around the Siha's fragrant thorn.
>
> I have a fawn from Aden's land,
>   On leafy buds and berries nursed;
> And you shall feed him from your hand,
>   Though he may start with fear at first.
> And I will lead you where he lies
>   For shelter in the noon-tide heat;
> And you may touch his sleeping eyes,
>   And feel his little silvery feet.

But the best evocations of the dreamlike element in childhood gardens are based, like Dean Hole's, on the magnification of real, particular objects. There is the same sense of particularity in this poem by John Clare:

> The stonecrop that on ruins comes
>   And hangs like golden balls—
> How oft to reach its shining blooms
>   We scaled the mossy walls!
> And weeds—we gathered weeds as well,
>   Of all that bore a flower,
> And tied our little posies up
>   Beneath the eldern bower.

J. S. Copley. The Little Gardener. c. 1790.

Pierre Auguste Renoir. Girl with a Watering-can. 1876.
Chester Dale Collection: Washington, National Gallery of Art.

> Our little gardens there we made
>   Of blossoms all arow,
> And though they had no roots at all
>   We hoped to see them grow;
> And in the cart rut after showers
>   Of sudden summer rain
> We filled our tiny waterpots
>   And cherished them in vain . . .

For the romantic mind there is an unfailing fascination in a deserted garden; and nowhere is this more vividly and evocatively expressed than in a simple children's story, published in 1911, but still read and re-read ardently by its devotees, whatever their age. Frances Hodgson Burnett's *The Secret Garden* describes how the walled garden in a great estate among the Yorkshire moors, kept locked and neglected since a tragic death, brought health and happiness to two children. One was the miserable, spoilt, and hypochondriac son of the woman whose memory was morbidly enshrined in the locked garden. The other was a weakly and at first friendless orphan girl brought home from India.

The girl, Mary, had been encouraged by the housekeeper to go skipping around the garden. Thus she had discovered the walled enclosure, but there seemed to be no way into it. Here was a puzzle to be solved. A robin whom Mary befriends in her loneliness shows her where the key is buried, and leads her to the hidden door in the wall.

> Mary had stepped close to the robin, and suddenly the gust of wind swung aside some loose ivy trails, and more suddenly still she jumped towards them and caught them in her hand. This she did because she had seen something under them—a round knob which had been covered by the leaves hanging over it. It was the knob of a door.
>
> She put her hands under the leaves and began to pull and push them aside. Thick as the ivy hung, it nearly all was a loose and swinging curtain, though some had crept over wood and iron. Mary's heart began to thump and her hands to shake a little in her delight and excitement. The robin kept singing and twittering away and tilting his head on one side, as if he were as excited as she was. What was this under her hands which was square and made of iron and which her fingers found a hole in?

It was the lock of the door which had been closed ten years, and she put her hand in her pocket, drew out the key, and found it fitted the keyhole. She put the key in and turned it. It took two hands to do it, but it did turn.

And then she took a long breath and looked behind her up the long walk to see if anyone was coming. No one was coming. No one ever did come, it seemed, and she took another long breath, because she could not help it, and she held back the swinging curtain of ivy and pushed back the door which opened slowly—slowly.

Then she slipped through it, and shut it behind her, and stood with her back against it, looking about her and breathing quite fast with excitement, and wonder, and delight.

She was standing *inside* the secret garden.

It was the sweetest, most mysterious-looking place anyone could imagine. The high walls which shut it in were covered with the leafless stems of climbing roses, which were so thick that they were matted together. Mary Lennox knew they were roses because she had seen a great many roses in India. All the ground was covered with grass of a wintry brown, and out of it grew clumps of bushes which were surely rose-bushes if they were alive. There were numbers of standard roses which had so spread their branches that they were like little trees. There were other trees in the garden, and one of the things that made the place look strangest and loveliest was that climbing roses had run all over them and swung down long tendrils which made light swaying curtains, and here and there they had caught at each other or at a far-reaching branch and had crept from one tree to another and made lovely bridges of themselves. There were neither leaves nor roses on them now, and Mary did not know whether they were dead or alive, but their thin grey or brown branches and sprays looked like a sort of hazy mantle spreading over everything, walls, and trees, and even brown grass, where they had fallen from their fastenings and run along the ground. It was this hazy tangle from tree to tree which made it look so mysterious. Mary had thought it must be different from other gardens which had not been left all by themselves so long; and, indeed, it was different from any other place she had ever seen in her life.

'How still it is!' she whispered. 'How still!'

Then she waited a moment and listened at the stillness. The robin, who had flown to his tree-top, was still as all the rest. He did not even flutter his wings; he sat without stirring and looked at Mary.

'No wonder it is still,' she whispered again, 'I am the first person who has spoken in here for ten years.'

She moved away from the door, stepping as softly as if she were afraid of awakening someone. She was glad that there was grass under her feet and that her steps made no sounds. She walked under one of the fairy-like arches between the trees and looked up at the tendrils and sprays which formed them.

'I wonder if they are all quite dead,' she said. 'Is it all a quite dead garden? I wish it wasn't.' . . .

But she was *inside* the wonderful garden, and she could come through the door under the ivy at any time, and she felt she had found a world all her own.

The sun was shining inside the four walls and the high arch of blue sky over this particular piece of Misselthwaite seemed even more brilliant and soft than it was over the moor. The robin flew down from his tree-top and hopped about or flew after her from one bush to another. He chirped a good deal and had a very busy air, as if he were showing her things. Everything was strange and silent, and she seemed to be hundreds of miles away from anyone, but somehow she did not feel lonely at all. All that troubled her was her wish that she knew whether all the roses were dead, or if perhaps some of them had lived and might put out leaves and buds as the weather got warmer. She did not want it to be a quite dead garden. If it were a quite alive garden, how wonderful it would be, and what thousands of roses would grow on every side!

Her skipping-rope had hung over her arm when she came in, and after she had walked about for a while she thought she would skip round the whole garden, stopping when she wanted to look at things. There seemed to have been grass paths here and there, and in one or two corners there were alcoves of evergreen with stone seats or tall moss-covered flower-urns in them.

As she came near the second of these alcoves she stopped skipping. There had once been a flower-bed in it, and she thought she saw something sticking out of the black earth—some sharp little pale green points. She remembered what Ben Weatherstaff had said, and she knelt down to look at them.

'Yes, they are tiny growing things and they *might* be crocuses or snowdrops or daffodils,' she whispered.

She bent very close to them and sniffed the fresh scent of the damp earth. . . .

At what point does the ideal garden take tangible shape as the real? The marginal territory has been poignantly explored in modern terms by Rumer Godden, in her story *An Episode of Sparrows*, which was re-created as a most moving film with the title *Innocent Sinners*. This story records the gardening ambitions and achievements of a London slum child, a girl of eleven, abandoned by her mother, who seeks to create her own little Eden in a graveyard beside a bombed church.

Loveday starts her gardening career by sowing some ordinary grass seed. Her sensations when she comes to the bombed site, after three weeks, and sees how Nature has collaborated with her, must, at one time or another, have been shared by every reader of this book:

> The packet had said that the seeds would come up, Mr Ibister had said that too; when Lovejoy had planted them she supposed she had believed it, but it had been more hope than belief. Now, on the patch of earth under the net, had come a film of green; when she bent down and looked closely, she could see that it was made of countless little stalks as fine as hairs, some so fine that she could scarcely see their colour, others vividly showing their new green. They're *blades*, thought Lovejoy, blades of grass! In the border were what she thought at first were tiny weeds, until she saw the real weeds among them. The weeds were among the grass too; she could tell them because they were bigger, a different pattern, and when she looked again the borders were peopled with myriad heads, all alike, each head made of two flat leaves, no bigger than pin-heads, on a stalk; they were so many and all the same, that she knew they were meant; no weed seeded like that. They must come from a sowing . . . my sowing, thought Lovejoy suddenly, the seeds *I* planted.
>
> She knelt down, carefully lifted the net away, and very gently, with her palm, she brushed the hair blades; they seemed to move as if they were not quite rooted, but rooted they were; when she held one in her thumb and finger, it did not come away. 'It's like . . . earth's fur,' said Lovejoy. . . .

Jean Jamson. Girl with a Basket. 1963. *Desmond Corcoran.*

Adam. c. 1178. Stained Glass. West window of the nave of Canterbury Cathedral.

2
Come, My Spade

'Come, my spade,' exclaimed the grave-digger in *Hamlet*, 'there is no ancient gentlemen but gardeners, ditchers, and grave-makers; they hold up Adam's profession.' Though Adam and his profession are so widely known, Holy Writ has very little to say of either, thus allowing each generation to fashion him in its own mould. One of the first to elaborate on Eden's inmates was Milton in *Paradise Lost*. He described one of the fundamental situations of gardeners: the wife telling the husband what to do.

> Adam, well may we labour still to dress
> This Garden, still to tend Plant, Herb and Flour,
> Our pleasant task enjoind, but till more hands
> Aid us, the work under our labour grows,
> Luxurious by restraint; what we by day
> Lop overgrown, or prune, or prop, or bind
> One night or two with wanton growth derides,
> Tending to wilde. Thou therefore now advise
> Or hear what to my mind first thoughts present,
> Let us divide our labours, thou where choice
> Leads thee, or where most needs, whether to wind
> The Woodbine round this Arbour, or direct
> The clasping Ivie where to climb, while I
> In yonder Spring of Roses intermixt
> With Myrtle, find what to redress till Noon:
> For while so near each other thus all day
> Our task we choose, what wonder if so near
> Looks intervene and smiles, or object new
> Casual discourse draw on, which intermits
> Our dayes work brought to little, though begun
> Early, and th'hour of Supper comes unearn'd.
> To whom mild answer Adam thus return'd . . .

The duties of Adam were described curtly but covered a multitude of activities: he was put into Eden to dress the garden and keep it. In 1618 William Lawson enlarged considerably on the work of the gardener:

> The gardener had not need be an idle or lazy lubber, forso your orchard, being a matter of such moment, will not prosper, there will ever be something to do. Weeds are always growing; the great Mother of all living creatures is full of seed in her bowels, and any stirring gives them heat of sun, and being laid near day, they grow: moles work daily, though not always alike: winter herbs at all times will grow (except in extreme frost). In winter your trees and herbs would be light'ned of snow, and your allies cleansed: drifts of snow will set deer, hares and conies, and other noysome beasts, over your walls and in your orchard. . . .

And when summer comes, the chores and responsibilities are multiplied. Finally, there is this advice:

> If you be not able, nor willing to hire a gardener, keep your profits to yourself, but then you must take all the pains.

A hurrying, scurrying scene of the gardener's activity, such as one sees—at a much earlier date—in a picture by Breughel, is to be found in the poem *De Hortibus* by the French Jesuit, René Rapin. 'I cannot therefore but wonder, that excellent Piece, so elegant, pleasant and instructive, should be no more enquired for,' wrote John Evelyn, who used its second book, 'made English by my late Son Evelyn', to conclude his *Silva*:

> And since the lawless Grass will oft invade
> The neighb'ring Walks, repress th' aspiring Blade,
> Suffer no Grass or rugged dirt t'impair
> Your smoother Paths. But to the Gard'ner's care
> These things we leave; they are his Business,
> With setting Flowers and planting fruitful Trees:
> And with the Master let the Servants join,
> With him their willing Hearts and Hands combine,
> Some should with Rowlers tame the yielding Ground,
> Making it plain where ruder Clods abound.
> Some may fit Moisture to your Meadows give,

And so the Plants and Gardens may derive
Refreshing streams; let others sweep away
The fallen Leaves; mend hedges that Decay:
Cut off superfluous Boughs; or with a Spade
Find where the Moles their winding Nests have made;
Then close them up. Another flowers may sow
In Beds prepar'd; on all some Task bestow;
That if the Master happens to come down,
To fly the Smoak and Clamour of the Town,
He in his Villa none may idle find,
But secret Joys may please his wearied Mind.

A number of authors in the late eighteenth and early nineteenth century defined and described the duties and attributes of a good gardener with more precision. J. C. Loudon in his *Encyclopaedia of Gardening*, first published in 1822, and for long the standard dictionary, summarized the opinions of such writers as Traugott Schwamstapper (whoever he might be) and the Rev W. Marshall, and his own views. A selection of the resulting precepts follows:

Decorum is the refinement of propriety. It is in order to procure stable-dung for hot-beds; it is proper to do this at all times when it is wanted, but it is *decorous* to have the work performed early in the morning, that the putrescent vapours and dropping litter may not prove offensive to the master of the garden, should he, or any of his family or friends, visit that scene.

Neatness, as opposed to slovenliness, is well understood; it consists in having every thing where it ought to be; and in attending to the decorum of finishing operations, and to minute things in general. These abstract hints may be considered as more particularly directed to master operators; the following practical directions apply both to masters and their journeymen or labourers.

Perform every operation in the proper season ...
Perform every operation in the best manner ...
Complete every part of an operation as you proceed ...
Finish one job before you begin another ...
In leaving off work at any job, leave your work and tools in an orderly manner ...

In leaving off work for the day, make a temporary finish, and carry your tools to the tool house . . .

In passing to and from your work, or, on any occasion, through any part of what is considered under the charge of the gardener, keep a vigilant look-out for weeds, decayed leaves, or any other deformity, and remove them, or some of them, in passing along. Attend to this particularly on walks, edgings and in passing through hot-houses, etc. In like manner, take off insects, or leaves infected by them. Much in large as well as in small gardens may be effected by this sort of timely or preventive attention, which induces suitable habits for a young gardener, and occupies very little time. . . .

Finally, attend to personal habits and cleanliness. Never perform any operation without gloves on your hands that you can do with gloves on; even weeding is far more effectually and expeditiously performed by gloves, the fore-fingers and thumbs of which terminate in wedge-like thimbles of steel, kept sharp. Most other operations may be performed with common gloves. Thus, no gardener need have hands like bears' paws. . . . Let your dress be clean, neat, simple and harmonious in form and colour: in your movements maintain an erect posture, easy and free gait and motion; let your manner be respectful and decorous to your superiors; and conduct fair and agreeable to your equals.

Elevate, meliorate, and otherwise improve, any raw, crude, harsh, or inharmonious features in your physiognomy, by looking often at the faces of agreeable people, by occupying your mind with agreeable and useful ideas, and by continually instructing yourself by reading. This will also give you features if you have none. Remember that you are paid and maintained by and for the use of and pleasure of your employer, who may no more wish to see a dirty, ragged, uncouth-looking, grinning, or conceited biped in his garden, than a starved, haggard, untutored horse in his stable.

What was it like to be a working gardener in one of the almost fabled gardens of the great past? Already, in 1700, 'Chatsworth, like a Sun in an hazy Air, adds Lustre to those Dusky Mountains, and attracts a general Congress of Spectators of its Wonders. . . .' In 1826 Joseph Paxton had been appointed head of the gardens, and before long it was again famed throughout the world for its wonders—having suffered a temporary period of decay. Robert Aughtie (1823–1901) joined the microcosm that centred round the Dukes of Devonshire, and went to work at Chatsworth. He kept a diary, unselfconsciously recording his daily activities. Today, reading in a matter-of-fact way of the daily life and some of the great occasions of this nineteenth-century Eden takes us back to a period that seems almost as remote as the days of Genesis. The following entries are for September 1848:

4. Monday. After breakfast went and saw over the Botanical gardens [in Sheffield]. There is a very good range of houses with some good plants. Stayed there some time, then went over the town again. Returned for tea and started for home at $\frac{1}{4}$ past 4 with Mrs Parker. Had a very pleasant journey. Got home a little after nine.
5. Tuesday. Was very fine all day—went partying.*
6. Wednesday. Was very busy all day raking the borders.
7. Thursday. Was very fine all day.
8. Friday. A most charming day—left work at five o'clock to join a party at Haddon hall. Went across the Park. Had some difficulty to find my way. When I got there I was surprised to find only a few there—about 28. Left about $\frac{1}{2}$ past 9. Walked home with Miss Stone through the park—was moonlight.
9. Saturday. Went to a footing supper at the wheat sheaf—Ingleby's—got there at 7. A most excellent supper was served consisting of roast beef, boiled leg of mutton, roast shoulder of veal, roast fowl, jugged hare, vegetables: Second course two plumb puddings, Derbyshire pudding and 7 fruit tarts. Eighteen sat down to dinner namely George, Fox, Fog, Wall, Dumbrill, Gillingham, Corbett, Arnison, Guildford, Ahearn, Taylor, Baker, Donald, Cromwell . . . Aughtie. Scott did not come in till afterwards. Was initiated in the Oddfellows club at Baslow.
10. Sunday. A drenching wet day. It commenced raining last evening about five and did not leave off till almost seven this evening. When it cleared up the moon shone and it turned to a frost. Went to chaple in the morning—rained all the way. Mr Spencer preached morning and evening. Dined with Mr J. Littlewood. Went with him in the afternoon to the church.

---

* That is, taking parties round the garden. These duties were arranged on a rota. As many as 600 people might come in a day.

11. Monday. Very busy taking away Musas and arranging the borders. Rather cold promises for a frost.
12. Tuesday. Fine all day with cold wind. Spraying the orange trees. Went partying. Wrote a letter to P. Hall.
13. Wednesday. Finished the large Wellington rock. Had some ale in the evening to christen it. Got rather tipsey and was very noisey coming home. The Duke arrived at Chatsworth. Very fine.
14. Thursday, 15. Friday. Very fine days.
15. Friday. The Duke and Duchess of Cambridge, the Duke of Wellington, the Duke and Duchess of Beaufort and D and Ds of . . . arrived at Chatsworth on a visit to the Duke of Devonshire. Was very fine all day. Got a sight of the ball room. Henry Slark came. Received a letter from P. Hall.
16. Saturday. Very busy getting the place ready for the company to see the gardens. They went round about noon. Received a letter from P. Hall. Wrote one to Henry. Took a walk along the 'four mile walk'.
17. Sunday. Went to Chaple returned to dinner. After dinner went to the Catholic chaple at Hassop. Found it very badly attended. Liked the manner and person of the priest very much. Went on to Bakewell. Took tea with the Heane's. Went to Chaple. Mr Spence preached at both services. A most delightful day. Mrs Wallace and her daughter went out for the day.
18. Monday. This evening the water works were illuminated and a large display of rockets. Was stationed at the ring pond. Rather foggy. A supper was given to the men. I did not stop as it was late.
19. Tuesday. The Duke and Ds. of Cambridge and the Duke of Wellington left Chatsworth. Went in the house in the afternoon and had tea in the still room with Henry Slark and Jane. Saw the dining rooms and drawing rooms lighted up. Also the library. Saw the ale cellars. Left a little before nine.

There is one type of gardener who plays an important part in gardening history but about which we know little. In the late eighteenth and early nineteenth century the English school of landscape design had become fashionable throughout Europe—particularly in France as *le jardin anglais*—and as far away as Russia. British gardeners were also during that period exceptionally skilful horticulturists and fruit growers. The Scots particularly found good posts, sometimes of considerable influence, in many aristocratic courts. Little is known of these men. Few, if any, kept diaries. Thomas Blaikie is an exception. Much of his working life was spent in France. He was very Scottish and his spelling was phonetic. Though popular with his clients, whom he obviously amused, he was blunt, outspoken, and, one feels, he never thought highly of most foreigners, who in turn entertained and amazed him. Much of the time he was abroad England and France were at war, yet he dealt regularly with British nurserymen such as James Lee of Hammersmith. Some years before, engaged by Drs Fothergill and Pitcairn, he had made the first organized British plant-collecting trip to the Swiss Alps. Though his description of that is graphic, it is better for our purpose to quote from his diary when he was giving us unconsciously brilliant pictures of France, at the time just before the Revolution—which he survived. In March 1783 he wrote:

> As the Court resided at St Cloud which was bought by the Queen from the Duke of Orleans the Compte Dartois came and lodged at Bagatelle; this gave little disturbance to the place as he arrived frequently very late or rather in the morning from St Cloud and Generally hardly went out before he set of for Diner and seemed to take very little notice of any thing, unless the melons which he took generally with him for the Queen who prefered those above all others; although all this distinction, this gave me little oppertunity of seeing the Compte; however one day in the Morning arrived Mme de Polignac [Comtesse Jules de Polignac] with some other ladys of honour of the Queens to see Bagatelle and as the Compte was not up they desired not to call him; after walking and viewing the Gardens and asking me Many questions about the Compte and whether or not I was contented with him, I answered judiciously that I was not and that I never saw a more Lazier and a Man of less taste and that he had not once come to see the Gardens since he Lodged there; this gave no little Sport and Laughter to those Ladys who returned and told the Queen all that I had said; this with perhaps some additional storys furnished Laughter enough for diner when the Compte Dartois arrived so that there whole discourse was mostly taken up about me and in the evening one of the footmen

who waited at table came and told me the whole Story and Said that Most likely his Highness would be angry with me for talking so lightly of him and as there was a sort of a hunting diner tomorrow I would most likely have a Sharp rebuke and some thought that it might go further, but as I knew I had said nothing of any consiquence I was very easy.

However, next Morning the great Company arrived and as I was walking with some of the noblemen the Compte D'Artois came out and seeing me at some distance called so that I went directly to him, so he asked me 'Well Blaikie are you not contented with me?' I told him no. 'Why so?' 'Because' says I 'there is no pleasure in working for you as I hardly know whether or not I please you as you never come to see the works after so much expences and as I wish to please you and that you should enjoy my works.' 'What' says he 'Is it only that? I promise I will come and see you oftener.' With that he took hold of my arm and walked all round the Garden. How this surprized the most of those that thought what I had said was of such a great crime and to See how those people caresses one that is in favour, for soon as the Comte had left Me and was gone in Severals of them came and complemented me, others beged of Me to Speak for them to the Comte as they said that I was so happy as that I could speak with freedom, others attributed it to that I was a Stranger and an Englishman and that there was more notice taken of me than people of the country; this way of reasoning created jealousy amongst Some of them; after this I was tolerable quitte although there was little new works done; a little after this we had a Visite of the grand duke and Duches of Rusia [later Paul I] who came and dined at Bagatelle with the Comte Dartois and the Queen.

This great Duke is very emproperly named as he may be called the little Duke as it is hardly possible to find a more little uglier man than him; however the Duches is a fine Woman tall and well made; they went all round the Gardens the grand Duches along with the Queen who seemed exceeding well pleased with the Gardens, the Queen asked me if I liked the French beter than I used to do this surprized the Duchess who asked why so and was not I a Frenchman? the Queen told her that I was English and added one of the best of that Country. This was no doubt flattering to Me to hear such aplause from persons of that rank; as all the noblemen stayed behind I ofered my hand to the Queen and grand Duches going into the Hermitage; this made the Rusian Ambassador run to take the hand of his Mistress and in his hurry he tumbled and fell into the River; this gave cause to a deal of Laughter and endeed I could not help although obliged to hide; however all passed well and the fete ended seemingly with great contentment on all Sides.

The social status and the functions of professional gardeners have varied very much at different times and in different places. Surely the most extraordinary gardeners were those seen by Sir Robert Ker Porter in Constantinople at the beginning of the last century:

> A set of persons called Bostangees, properly a corps of gardeners for the Seraglio, present a most ludicrous costume. They have two employments besides that of horticulture; first, guarding the person of the sovereign; second, seizing criminals, and dragging them to justice. But their beacon-heads, when seen from afar, ought to be sufficient warning to the latter objects to keep out of their way; their caps being constructed of scarlet cloth, rising high in a cylindrical form, then suddenly making an acute angle to the front or rear, like the machine called a *cow* on our refractory chimneys. The dress on these men is richly embroidered, and covered on the breast with lumps of embossed silver. Their daggers, or yaltagars, are also very splendid.

The extra duties of these Bostangees were quite unusual even for gardeners, who are so often jacks of all trades. We may recall that George London, gardener to Bishop Compton who had one of the most remarkable gardens in England at Fulham Palace, went so far beyond his normal duties as to play a key part in the escape of Princess Anne, engineered by the Duchess of Marlborough and his employer.

By force of circumstances gardeners and gardening came late to North America. There were isolated Spanish settlements, but little else. J. C. Loudon could not find any American gardens to illustrate in his *Encyclopaedia*, and supplied only a picture of a settlement. In 1828 the *Gardener's Magazine* received a rather despondent communication from Mr Jesse Buell, a corresponding member of the Horticultural Society of London, on the state of gardening in his native country:

> Horticulture received but little attention in the United States, until quite a recent period; and with occasional exceptions, was limited to

the culture of common culinary vegetables and fruits. A young people must earn the means of procuring the luxuries and elegances of horticultural refinement, before they can enjoy them. The wants and necessities of a new country are generally too imperious to leave much time, or to afford adequate means, for indulging extensively in the ornamental and scientific departments of gardening; and perhaps the republican principles of the government, and the habits of the people, have in a measure tended to retard improvement in these higher branches. . . .

But the greatest obstacle to improvement has been the want of prominent examples. There have been no royal gardens, no botanical gardens (but in name), no public gardens, to stimulate and instruct those who might wish to cultivate taste, or acquire knowledge in this branch of rural improvement. Respectable private gardens were occasionally found in the neighbourhood of large towns; but their number was too small, and the access to them too limited, to produce much influence towards general improvement.

This, surely, was an exaggeratedly gloomy, or very localized view of the situation. The European 'curious' gardener—curious in the sense that he was of a serious, enquiring, and experimental turn of mind— had already been represented by the eminent John Bartram whose reciprocal arrangements with a variety of correspondents had resulted in the introduction of many American plants to Europe and *vice versa*, and who established a celebrated botanical garden at Philadelphia. He had died full of years in 1777, to be succeeded by his son.

Thomas Jefferson, third President of the United States of America, was an ardent botanist and an active pioneer of American horticulture. His garden at Monticello—from which his work often divorced him for long periods—was famous far beyond his native soil, and in it were grown plants from many parts of the world. He travelled in Europe and maintained a considerable horticultural correspondence and exchange of plants with nurserymen. When, in 1792, he was Secretary of State, the genus *Jeffersonia* was named in his honour—no hollow tribute.

His *Garden Book* survives and has been published—a record of facts kept from 1766 to 1824—and also a great deal of his horticultural correspondence. It is to this last that we may turn to see the true gardener that lay under the versatile man of affairs. In 1811, when he was sixty-eight, his deep feelings on the craft of gardening were expressed to Charles Willson Peale in these downright terms:

> I have often thought that if heaven had given me choice of my position and calling, it should have been on a rich spot of earth, well watered, and near a good market for the productions of the garden. No occupation is so delightful to me as the culture of the earth, and no culture comparable to that of the garden. Such a variety of subjects, some one always coming to perfection, the failure of one thing repaired by the success of another, and instead of one harvest a continued one through the year. Under a total want of demand except for our family table, I am still devoted to the garden. But though an old man, I am but a young gardener.

His constant preoccupation with his garden at Monticello is shown again and again in his letters, particularly to his family. In June 1790 he wrote from New York—a note of homesickness is always present— to his daughter Maria:

> We had not peas or strawberries here till the 8th day of this month. On the same day I heard the first whip-poor-will whistle. Swallows and martins appeared here on the 21st of April. When did they appear with you? and when had you peas, strawberries and whip-poor-will in Virginia? Take notice hereafter whether the whip-poor-will always come with the strawberries and peas. . . .

She dutifully replies, delicately hinting that she is really rather busy:

> We had peas the 10th May, and strawberries the 17th of the same month, though not in that abundance we are accustomed to, in consequence of a frost this spring. As for the martins, swallows, and the whip-pur-wills, I was so taken up with my chickens that I never noticed them. . . .

An example typical of many letters that he wrote to horticultural correspondents is one to Benjamin Hawkins in 1792 (at that time, remember, he was busy with the affairs of Secretary of State):

At Mrs Trist's desire, I forward you about a dozen beans of three different kinds, having first taken toll of them as she had done before. They are of the scarlet flowering kind. This is all I know of them. The most beautiful bean in the world is the Caracalla bean which, though in England a greenhouse plant, will grow in the open air in Virginia and Carolina. I never could get one of these in my life.

In that year he wrote from Philadelphia to his other daughter, Martha, now married:

I suppose you are busy in your garden. Shackleford promised me *on his honour* to cover it with manure, has he done it? if not, tell him I have written to enquire.

Martha replied with a long letter that must have delighted her father:

. . . You will see that I am a much better gardener than last year tho' in truth old George is so slow that I shall never shine in that way without your assistance. Tom has been a man of honour with respect to the manure. We have had some very high winds lately one of which blew down 5 trees, in and about the grove and did some other mischief. It was accompanied with severe lightning. The noise of the wind kept us from hearing anything of the thunder except when it was extremely bad. We have discovered a very beautiful tree near the lower round a bout, a silver fir I believe. It differs from the common pine in having a smooth green bark and the bottom of their leaves white and much smoother than the others . . .

It is sad to recall that when Jefferson died, he was not well off, and Monticello, to which he had devoted so much of his life, and where he had collected so many plants, was sold.

The speedy progress of American gardening is marked by the year 1852, when Andrew Jackson Downing died prematurely (and with courage) as the consequence of a needless shipping disaster. Still a young man, he yet had established an international reputation as the first American landscape artist, and one able to work in the grand manner. A decade or so before he died he had enunciated his guiding principles:

The embellishment of nature, which we call Landscape Gardening, springs naturally from a love of country life, an attachment to a certain spot, and a desire to render that place attractive—a feeling which seems more or less strongly fixed in the minds of all men. But we should convey a false impression, were we to state that it may be applied with equal success to residences of every class and size, in the country. Lawn and trees, being its two essential elements, some of the beauties of Landscape Gardening may, indeed, be shown wherever a wood or grass surface and half-a-dozen trees are within our reach; we may even with such scanty space, have tasteful grouping, varied surface, and agreeably curved walks; but our art, to appear to advantage, requires some extent of surface—its lines should lose themselves indefinitely, and unite agreeably and gradually with those of the surrounding country.

In the case of large landed estates, its capabilities may be displayed to their full extent, as from fifty to five hundred acres may be devoted to a park or pleasure grounds. Most of its beauty and all its charms, may, however, be enjoyed in ten or twenty acres, fortunately situated, and well treated; and Landscape Gardening, in America, combined and working in harmony as it is with our fine scenery, is already beginning to give us results scarcely less beautiful than those produced by its finest effects abroad. The lovely villa residences of our noble river and lake margins, when well treated—even in a few acres of tasteful foreground—seem so entirely to appropriate the whole adjacent landscape, and to mingle so sweetly in their outlines with the woods, the valleys and the shores around them, that the effects are often truly enchanting.

The later editions of this work include a touching and unsophisticated epitaph, written by 'his literary friend George William Curtis':

In the afternoon, they brought him home, and laid him in his library. A terrific storm burst over the river and crashed among the hills, and the wild sympathy of nature surrounded that blasted home. But its master lay serene in the peace of the last prayer he uttered. Loving hands had woven garlands of the fragrant blossoms of the Cape jessamine, the sweet clematis, and the royal roses he loved so well. The next morning was calm and bright, and he was laid in the grave-yard, where his father and mother lie. The quiet Fishkill mountains, that were the love of the shy boy in the garden, now watch the grave of the man, who was buried, not yet thirty-seven years old, but with great duties done in this world, and with firm faith in the divine goodness.

> Unwatch'd, the garden bough shall sway,
>   The tender blossoms flutter down,
>   Unloved, that beech will gather brown,
> This maple burn itself away.
>
> Unloved, the sun-flower shining fair
>   Ray round with flame her disk of seed,
>   And many a rose carnation feed
> With summer spice the humming air.
>
> Unloved, by many a sandy bar
>   The brook shall babble down the plain,
>   At noon, or when the lesser wain
> Is twisting round the polar star;
>
> Uncared for, gird the windy grove,
>   And flood the haunts of hern and crake;
>   Or into silver arrows break,
> The sailing moon in creek and cove . . .
>
> Till from the garden and the wild
>   A fresh association blow,
>   And year by year the landscapes grow
> Familiar to the stranger's child;
>
> As year by year, the labourer tills
>   His wonted glebe, or lops the glades;
>   And year by year our memory fades
> From all the circle of the hills.

Soon after Downing died Emerson was able to publish his quatrain showing the American gardener as a dedicated man:

> True Brahmin, in the morning meadows wet,
>   Expound the Vedas on the violet,
> Or, hid in vines, peeping through many a loop,
>   See the plum redden, and the beurré stoop.

THE GARDENER AS SYMBOL

The gardener has often been a symbol of certain essential elements in life. He appears in the York and Coventry Mystery Plays. Sacheverell Sitwell has portrayed him in a shimmering picture:

> Stand still, sun, let the summer day burn slow,
> For I must snare the gardener with a stretch of notes,
> Catch him alive with words as in a web.
> O, brittle cage to hold back such a throat of fire!
> I build the bars now for his wings to beat on;
> See, I hold him prisoner!
> His wide hat cooler than a whole tree's shade
> Like the snow cap on a mountain shelters him:
> As he bows among the flowerbeds in the beating sun
> The leaves are fanning him
> Like the cool flow of stars above the hot sun's face,
> Dancing trees for running water,
> Mute as me for speech,
> And yet his throat were like a nightingale's
> Had he but power to sing:
> Like a boat's neck on the water should he ride in air
> On those slow tides, the summer winds—
> He shall float among the boughs where birds are singing
> As light as wind who sighs in the cornfield
> And, at night, lies hid in leaves:
> Till those plumes come,
> He will pace his Kingdom by loud starlight
> On tiptoe past the windows
> Listening to the harp's loud beat,
> In case a sash should open while music masks the noise,
> And Cherubino, like a flash of stars, be gone again.

Richard Church transfers him momentarily to another world:

> Lifting through the broken clouds there shot
> A searching beam of golden sunset-shine.
> It swept the town allotments, plot by plot,
> And all the digging clerks became divine—
> Stood up like heroes with their spades of brass,
> Turning the ore that made the realms of Spain!
> So shone they for a moment. Then, alas!
> The cloud-rift closed; and they were clerks again.

One of the most generous and eloquent of tributes to the gardener's temperament is that of Gerald Bullett:

> Gardeners are good. Such vices as they have
> Are like the warts and bosses in the wood
> Of an old oak. They're patient, stubborn folk,
> As needs must be whose busyness it is
> To tutor wildness, making war on weeds.
> With slow sagacious words and knowing glance
> They scan the sky, do all that mortals may
> To learn civility to pesty birds
> Come after new green peas, cosset and prune
> Roses, wash with lime the orchard trees,
> Make sun-parlours for seedlings.
> >   Patient, stubborn.
> Add cunning next, unless you'd put it first;
> For while to dig and delve is all their text
> There's cunning in their fingers to persuade
> Beauty to bloom and riot to run right,
> Mattock and spade, trowel and rake and hoe
> Being not tools to learn by learning rules
> But extra limbs these husbands of the earth
> Had from their birth. Of malice they've no more
> Than snaring slugs and wireworms will appease,
> Or may with ease be drowned in mugs of mild.
> Wherefore I say again, whether or no
> It is their occupation makes them so,
> Gardeners are good, in grain.

The craft of gardening seems inheritable, often passing from father to son and beyond; indeed, there are firms of family nurserymen still prospering in their fifth generation and possibly more. None has surpassed in distinction the historic family of Tradescants—who, in spite of their exotic-sounding name, were good East Anglians. John the elder first achieved fame when he travelled the Continent collecting rarities as gardener to the Earl of Salisbury during the building of Hatfield House at the beginning of the seventeenth century. He was concerned as an early financer of Virginian trading enterprises, thereby obtaining plants from that country. He went to Russia, whence he brought more plants and

Sir Stanley Spencer, RA. Gardening. 1945. *Leeds, City Art Gallery.*

S^r. John Tradescant Junr.
in his Garden.

Attributed to Emanuel de Critz. Sir John Tradescant, Junr., in his Garden. c. 1630.
Oxford, Ashmolean Museum.

where he attempted the compilation of the first flora of that country. As a 'gentleman adventurer' (a superior form of pirate) he botanized and collected plants in Algeria—or as it was more pleasantly called, the Barbary Coast. When employed by the Duke of Buckingham he used this royal favourite's influence to persuade His Majesty's ships to bring back plants. Finally, he settled down as royal gardener and at his home began a museum of oddities which he called his Ark. This was surrounded by a garden with a collection of rare trees, shrubs, and plants. This remarkable man can be seen figured in a carving on the stairway of Hatfield House.

When he died in 1637 his son was away in Virginia collecting plants. This second John returned to succeed his father as royal gardener and continued adding to the Ark. He was unmolested during the Cromwellian years. When he died in 1662 his son, also a gardener and the third John, had pre-deceased him. The Ark went to the antiquary Elias Ashmole and thence to the University of Oxford to become that greatest treasury of delights, the Ashmolean, where there is a fine portrait of John the Second attributed to Emanuel de Critz.

Few gardening families can have contributed more to the craft of gardening, and indeed to the fine cultural background of the Restoration age. The three John's were celebrated—with reference to the queens two of them in turn served—by some unknown writer of a faultless epitaph:

> Know, stranger, e'er thou pass, beneath this stone
> Lie John Tradescant, grandsire, father, son.
> These famous antiquarians that had been
> Both gardeners to the rose and lily Queen,
> Transplanted now themselves, sleep here; and when
> Angels shall with their trumpets waken men,
> And fire shall purge the world, these hence shall rise
> And change their gardens for a Paradise.

As a complement to this tribute here is a twentieth-century description of one of the last of Adam's breed to show a mastery over plants by means of inherited skill and instinct rather than textbook science and instruction. The scene is England, the garden is in Kent:

Honour the gardener! that patient man
Who from his schooldays follows up his calling,
Starting so modestly, a little boy
Red-nosed, red-fingered, doing what he's told,
Not knowing what he does or why he does it,
Having no concept of the larger plan,
But gradually, (if the love be there,
Irrational as any passion, strong,)
Enlarging vision slowly turns the key
And swings the door wide open on the long
Vistas of true significance. No more
Is toil a vacant drudgery, when purport
Attends each small and conscientious task,
—As the stone-mason setting yard by yard
Each stone in place, exalting not his gaze
To measure growth of structure, or assess
That slow accomplishment, but in the end
Tops the last finial and, stepping back
To wipe the grit for the last time from eyes,
Sees that he built a temple,—so the true
Born gardener toils with love that is not toil
In detailed time of minutes, hours, and days,
Months, years, a life of doing each thing well;
The Life-line in his hand not rubbed away
As you might think, by constant scrape and rasp,
But deepened rather, as the line of Fate,
By earth imbedded in his wrinkled palm;
A golden ring worn thin upon his finger,
A signet ring, no ring of human marriage,
On that brown hand, dry as a crust of bread,
A ring that in its circle belts him close
To earthly seasons, and in its slow thinning
Wears out its life with his.
That hand, that broke with tenderness and strength
Clumps of the primrose and the primula,
Watched by a loving woman who desired
Such tenderness and strength to hold her close,
And take her passionate giving, as he held
His broken plants and set them in the ground,
New children; but he had no thought of her.

She only stood and watched his capable hand
Brown with the earth and golden with the ring,
And knew her part was small in his lone heart.

So comes he at the last to that long Paradise
Where grateful Pharaoh hews a mountain tomb
For the good gardener, the faithful slave,
(Slave not of royalty, but his own piety,)
Painting the vaulted roof of that deep cave
With fresco of imperishable fruit
Such as no earthly gardener ever grew,
Pale peaches and pale grapes, so healthy-heavy
Yet slung from tendrils of a filament
Too weak to bear a locust's weight. He sleeps,
No pest, no canker troubling that deep sleep
Under the pattern that he scarce divined.

Victoria Sackville-West, who wrote those lines, was one of the great English gardeners, but women have gardened from the days of Eve, whose allocation of duties to Adam we have already mentioned. The woman of the household was traditionally in charge of the herbs and flower plots. In the sixteenth century Thomas Tusser wrote:

In Marche and in Aprill, from morning to night:
    in sowing and setting, good huswives delight;
To have in a garden, or other like plot:
    to trim up their house, and to furnish their pot.

Professionally women gardeners have principally been employed as weeders; again and again we find their wages entered in old account books. One at least became famous. When Celia Fiennes visited the Duke of Bedford's garden at Woburn in 1697 she passed into a cherry garden 'in the midst of which stands a figure of stone resembling an old weeder woman used in the garden, and my Lord would have her Effigie which is done so like and her clothes so well that at first I took it to be a real living body'.

An apologia for gardening as a pastime for women came, a little surprisingly, in the middle of the eighteenth century, from that lady of wit and fashion, Lady Mary Wortley Montagu, in a letter to her daughter:

I am really as fond of my garden as a young author of his first play, when it has been well received by the town, and can no more forbear teasing my acquaintance for their approbation. . . .

Gardening is certainly the next amusement to reading; and as my sight will now permit me little of that, I am glad to form a taste that can give me so much employment, and be the plaything of my age, now my pen and needle are almost useless to me.

The divorce of women from the genteel aspects of gardening that seems to have become complete in the late eighteenth and early nineteenth centuries is shown by a delightful passage in the memoir of Thomas Bewick, the singular naturalist and wood engraver. Writing in 1822 he said:

If I could influence the fair sex, there is one thing to which I would draw their attention; and that is Horticulture; and, connected with this, I would recommend them, as far as convenient, to become Florists, as this delightful and healthy employment—which has been long enough in the rude hands of men—would entice them into the open air, stimulate them to exertion and draw them away from their sedentary modes of life, mewed up in close rooms, where they are confined like nuns. This would contribute greatly to their amusement, and exhilarate their spirits. Every sensible man should encourage the fair sex to follow this pursuit. What would this world be without their help, to alleviate its burdens? It would appear a barren waste. It would no longer be a wide-spread garden of Eden, nor an earthly paradise within the reach of our enjoyments. May the fruits and flowers of it, reared and presented by their fair hands, ever operate as a charm in ensuring the attentions and unabating regard of all men! And of all good men it will.

Not long after Bewick wrote this women took to gardening in a much more general way. They were greatly encouraged to do so by the writings and example of Jane Loudon, helped by her husband John, the encyclopaedist. Both had great influence in North America, where Athens, Georgia, is said to have established, in 1890, the first Ladies Garden Club.

Women Gardeners. Detail of fifteenth-century French tapestry.
Paris, Musée du Louvre.

Johann Joachim Kändler. Harlequin and a Lady. Meissen porcelain group. c. 1760.
Mounted on Louis XV ormolu base, supporting a metal trellis–work arbour.
London, Antique Porcelain Company.

3

Fantasia of Flowers

Flowers have probably inspired more poets to flights of fancy than any other objects of Nature. The very word 'anthology' means, literally, 'a gathering of flowers'; and an anthology of notable poems about flowers would run to enough volumes to fill a window-box. In trying to illustrate in small compass the peculiar delights of flowers all one can do is to pick blooms of a few familiar species and consider some of the less familiar fancies which they have evoked in the minds of men and women of letters.

The presentation of flowers as a token of admiration, gratitude, or love originated, no doubt, in the Garden of Eden. It reached its peak of sophistication in the eighteenth century, when the association of flowers and flirtation, of adoration and the arbour, was commemorated not only in verse but in porcelain and printed wallpapers, in paintings by Boucher, enamels on patch-boxes, and embroidery on waistcoats. Here are some verses on this theme, written not by a man but a woman, Anna Laetitia Barbauld:

> Flowers to the fair: to you these flowers I bring,
> And strive to greet you with an earlier spring.
> Flowers, sweet and gay and delicate like you,
> Emblems of innocence and beauty too.
> With flowers the Graces bind their yellow hair,
> And flowery wreaths consenting lovers wear.
> Flowers, the sole luxury which nature knew,
> In Eden's pure and guiltless garden grew.
> To loftier form are rougher tasks assign'd;
> And sheltering oak resists the stormy wind,
> The tougher yew repels invading foes,
> And the tall pine for future navies grows;

But this soft family to caves unknown,
Were born for pleasure and delight alone;
Gay without toil and lovely without art,
They spring to cheer the sense, and glad the heart.
Nor blush, my fair, to own you copy these,
Your best, your sweetest empire is—to please.

To please. . . . These verses present one aspect of garden flowers: the rococo, the sentimental, perhaps the feminine view. There is another view—and, judging by those who have expressed it, apparently a male outlook—the rich, baroque excitement of the true florist.

The florist was, like the jeweller or the potter, more concerned with ornament than sentiment, and nowhere has this been shown more surely, over three hundred years and more, than in the cult of the metallic and geometric auricula. The Rev Samuel Gilbert, in 1683, celebrated the auricula—the Bear's Ear, as he called it, from a resemblance in the shape of the leaf—in lines which clearly express the florist's point of view:

See how the Bears Eares in their several dresses,
(That yet no Poet's pen to hight expresses.)
Each head adornèd with such rich attire,
Which Fools and Clowns may slight, whilst skil'd admire.
Their gold, their purples, scarlets, crimson dyes,
Their dark and lighter hair'd diversities.
With all their pretty shades and Ornaments,
Their parti-colour'd coats and pleasing scents.
Gold laid on scarlet, silver on the blew
With sparkling eyes to take the eyes of you.
Mixt colours, many more to please that sense,
Other with rich and great magnificence,
In double Ruffs, with gold and silver laced,
On purple crimson and so neatly placed.
Ransack Flora's wardrobes, none sure can bring
More taking Ornaments t' adorn the spring.

A third approach to floral delights is that by way of Science—a study that has regrettably been omitted so far from this book as being an undelightful and sometimes rather smelly thing. But a little botany is good for us, particularly if we are old-fashioned and revert to the days when it was ruled over by a goddess, as it was as lately as the end of the eighteenth century. Charlotte Smith was impelled to address one of her *Elegiac Sonnets* to this deity in 1797:

> Of folly weary, shrinking from the view
> Of violence and fraud, allow'd to take
> All peace from humble life; I would forsake
> Their haunts for ever, and, sweet Nymph, with you
> Find shelter; where my tired, and tear-swoln eyes
> Among your silent shades of soothing hue,
> Your 'bells and florets of unnumber'd dyes'
> Might rest—And learn the bright varieties
> That from your lovely hands are fed with dew;
> And every veined leaf, that trembling sighs
> In mead or woodland; or in wilds remote,
> Or lurk with mosses in the humid caves,
> Mantle the cliffs, on dimpling rivers float,
> Or stream from coral rocks beneath the Ocean waves.

But already the pedantry of botany was under fire. We find these sharp words on botanical nomenclature in the introduction to *Letters on the Elements of Botany Addressed to a Lady*, written by no less a person than Jean-Jacques Rousseau:

> Hitherto Linnaeus had indeed determined the greatest part of known plants, but he had not named them; for defining a thing is not naming it, a phrase can never be a true name, nor can it come into common use. He provided against this defect by the invention of trivial names, which he joined to the generical ones in order to distinguish the species. By this contrivance the name of every plant is composed only of two words, which alone when chosen with discernment, and applied with propriety, often make the plant better known than the long phrases of Micheli and Plukenet. . . .
> Nothing is more pedantic or ridiculous, when a woman, or one of those men who resemble women, are asking you the name of an herb or flower in a garden, than to be under the necessity of answering by a long file of Latin words that have the appearance of a magical incantation; an inconvenience sufficient to deter such

FANTASIA OF FLOWERS

frivolous persons from a charming study offered with so pedantic an apparatus.

In our own century, stirred presumably by the same impulse as Rousseau, Robert Frost has addressed these charming lines to 'The Rose Family':

> The rose is a rose,
> And was always a rose.
> But the theory now goes
> That the apple's a rose,
> And the pear is, and so's
> The plum, I suppose.
> The dear only knows
> What will next prove a rose.
> You, of course, are a rose—
> But were always a rose.

But before discarding the scientific approach let us consider a few words about that basic element in gardening, the soil. Here are a few lines written in the eighteenth century by Dr James Grainger, author of *The Sugar-Cane*:

> Of composts shall the Muse descend to sing,
> Nor soil her heavenly plumes? The sacred Muse
> Naught sordid deems, but what is base; naught fair
> Unless true Virtue stamp it with her seal.
> Then, Planter, wouldst thou double thy estate
> Never, ah, never be asham'd to tread
> Thy dung-heaps.

And let us spare half a page for that valuable adjunct to scientific gardening, the magnifying-glass, as described in loving lines of near verse in 1709 by John Philips:

> She found the polish'd Glass, whose small Convex
> Enlarges to ten Millions of Degrees
> The Mite, invisible else, of Nature's Hand
> Least Animal; and shews, what Laws of Life
> The Cheese-Inhabitants observe, and how

Fabrick their Mansions in the harden'd Milk,
Wonderful Artists! But the hidden Ways
Of Nature would'st thou know? how first she frames
All things in Miniature? thy Specular Orb
Apply to well-dissected Kernels; lo!
Strange Forms arise, in each a little Plant
Unfolds its Boughs: observe the slender Threads
Of first-beginning Trees, their Roots, their Leaves,
In narrow Seeds describ'd . . .

From science it is but a short step to philosophy and Edmund Burke's *Inquiry into . . . the Sublime and Beautiful* which, on its appearance in 1756, was read by every gardener who was a cultured gentleman. We may choose that section wherein he shows that 'Proportion is not the Cause of Beauty in Vegetables':

Turning our eyes to the vegetable creation, we find nothing there so beautiful as flowers; but flowers are of almost every sort of shape, and of every sort of disposition; they are turned and fashioned into an infinite variety of forms; and from these forms botanists have given them their names, which are almost as various. What proportions do we discover between the stalks and the leaves of flowers, or between the leaves and pistils?

How does the slender stalk of the rose agree with the bulky head under which it bends? But the rose is a beautiful flower; and can we undertake to say that it does not owe a great deal of its beauty even to that disproportion: the rose is a large flower, yet it grows upon a small shrub; the flower of the apple is very small and grows upon a large tree; yet the rose and the apple blossom are both beautiful, and the plants that bear them are most engagingly attired, notwithstanding this disproportion. . . .

I grant that we may observe, in many flowers, something of a regular figure, and of a methodical disposition of the leaves. The rose has such a figure and such a disposition of its petals; but in an oblique view, when this figure is in good measure lost, and the order of the leaves confounded, it yet retains its beauty; the rose is even more beautiful before it is full blown; in the bud, before the exact figure is formed; and this is not the only instance wherein method and exactness, the soul of proportion, are found rather prejudicial than serviceable to the cause of beauty.

With this philosophical flourish by Burke we come to the first of the flowers—indeed the recognized Queen of Flowers—whose influence upon Fancy and Imagination is the main theme of this chapter. Let us first consider the original distinction between the red rose and the white, which has been a perennial subject of argument and analogy for poets and lovers, mediaeval barons and county cricketers. Here is William Drummond writing on this matter early in the seventeenth century:

> Flowre, which of Adon's blood
> Sprang, when of that cleare Flood,
> Which Venus wept, an other white was borne,
> The sweet Cynarean Youth thou right dost show;
> But this sharpe-pointed Thorne,
> Which doth (so prowde) about thy Crimson grow,
> What doth it represent?
> Boar's Tuskes (perhaps) his snowie Flancke which rent:
> O Show of Showes! of unesteemed Worth,
> Which both what kill'd and what was kill'd sett'st forth.

A characteristic amorous exercise on the colour theme is William Somervile's poem on 'Presenting to a Lady a White Rose and a Red', published in 1727:

> If this pale rose offend your sight
>   It in your bosom wear
> 'Twill blush to find itself less white,
>   And turn Lancastrian there.
>
> But, Celia, should the red be chose,
>   With gay vermilion bright,
> 'Twould sicken at each blush that glows
>   And in despair turn white . . .

Another treatment of the same theme is to be found in a poem by a little-known lyric poet of the early eighteenth century, John Smith:

> Go, lovely pair of roses, go,
>   This clad in scarlet, that in snow.
> Go, say to my ungentle fair,
>   (If on your forms she deigns to gaze)

You dare not hope to rival her,
    Or match the glories of her face;
But that you're humbly sent to prove
A youth undone by beauty and her love.

The sickly white in this pale rose
My wan and meager looks disclose;
But that which shines so fiercely bright,
    Whose head in painted flames aspires,
And blushes so with purple light,
    It seems to send forth real fires,
Tell her that rose's ruddy fires impart
The flames her eyes have kindled in my heart.

The scent of the rose is exquisitely evoked in one of Patrick Carey's *Trivial Poems and Triolets*, written in 1651, but not published until a hundred and sixty years later:

I smelt and prays'd the fragrant rose,
Blushing, thus answer'd she:
    The praise you gave,
    The scent I have,
    Doe not belong to mee;
This harmlesse odour, none
But only God indeed does owne;
To be his keepers, my poor leaves he chose;
And thus reply'd the rose . . .

Then there are William Hammond's gentle lines, written four years later, and inscribed 'To my dear Sister, Mrs S., on the Death of my dear Brother, Mr H. S. drowned':

After the honey drops of pearly showers,
    Urania walk'd to gather flowers:
Sweet Rose (I heard her say) why are these fears?
    Are these drops on thy cheek thy tears?
By those thy beauty fresher is, thy smell
    Arabian spices doth excel.

This rain (the Rose replied) feeds and betrays
    My odours; adds and cuts off days:
Had I not spread my leaves to catch this dew,
    My scent had not invited you.

Urania sigh'd, and softly said, 'Tis so,
    Showers blow the rose, and ripen woe;
For mine, alas, when washt in floods sweet clean,
    Heaven put his hand forth, and did glean.

Although the rose has never lost her throne in the Court of Flowers there was a period in the seventeenth century when her rule was seriously challenged. Anyone who has made a study of the Dutch and Flemish flower paintings of this period will have observed that the artists were almost as much attracted by the tulip as by the rose. It happened, of course, that this was the era of *Tulpenwoede*, or Tulipomania, when Dutch florists became obsessed with tulip breeding, invested huge sums of money in it, and persuaded everyone in the Low Countries who had even a few yards of back garden to cultivate the tulip. In every town there was a tavern where a 'collegium' or club for trading in tulips was set up, and in a single town during the years 1634–7, when the mania was at its height, deals to the value of ten million pounds sterling were made. No wonder the painters crammed a full quota of tulips into their already crowded floral compositions.

The vogue of the tulip reached Britain a little later, and in 1660 we find Thomas Fuller, in his *Antheologia, or the Speech of Flowers*, referring in picturesque terms to the tulip's challenge to the rose. One spring, in a small scantlin of ground there assembled 'yellow marigolds, wallflowers, auriculusses, gold knobs, and abundance of other nameless flowers, which would pose a nomenclator to call them by their distinct denominations'.

In this solemn randevoux of flowers and herbs, the Rose stood forth, and made an oration to this effect.

It is not unknown to you, how I have precedency of all flowers, confirmed unto me under the patent of a double sence, sight and smell. What more curious colours? how do all diers blush, when they behold my blushing as conscious to themselves that their art

Ambrosius Bosschaert (1565-1621). Vase with Flowers.
The Hague, Mauritshuis Museum.

Paul Cézanne (1839-1906). Tulips. *U.S.A., Private Collection.*

cannot imitate that tincture, which nature hath stamped upon me. Smell, it is not lusciously offensive, nor dangerously faint, but comforteth with a delight, and delighteth with the comfort thereof: yea, when dead, I am more soveraigne than living: what cordials are made of my syrups? how many corrupted lungs (those fans of nature) sore wasted with consumption that they seem utterly unable any longer to cool the heat of the heart, with their ventilation, are with conserves made of my stamped leaves, restored to their former soundness again. More would I say in my own cause, but that happily I may be taxed of pride, and selfe-flattery, who speake much in mine own behalf, and therefore I leave the rest to the judgement of such as hear me, and pass from this discourse to my just complaint.

There is lately a flower (shall I call it so? in courtesie I will tearme it so, though it deserve not the appellation) a Toolip, which hath engrafted the love and affections of most people unto it; and what it this Toolip? a well complexion'd stink, an ill favour wrapt up in pleasant colours; as for the use thereof in physick, no physitian hath honoured it yet with the mention, nor with a Greek, or Latin name, so inconsiderable hath it hitherto been accompted; and yet this is that which filleth all gardens, hundred of pounds being given for the root thereof, whilst I the Rose, am neglected and contemned, and conceived beneath the honour of noble hands, and fit only to grow in the gardens of yeomen.

Though the tulip has certainly been honoured by artists from Ambrosius Bosschaert to Cézanne, and after, the poets have hardly done justice to it. It is mentioned nowhere in classical literature. Its peculiar form, however, was perfectly epitomized in a few lines by Humbert Wolfe:

Clean as a lady,
Cool as glass,
Fresh without fragrance
The tulip was.

The craftsman who carved her
Of metal, prayed:
'Live, oh thou lovely!'
Half metal she stayed.

Lest we inadvertently leave the impression that the 'metallic' flower has little emotional appeal, and has always been chiefly valued for the amount of gold or 'brass' that it produced, we should recall the extraordinary passion for the tulip that gripped the artisan florists of the Midlands and the north of England in the early nineteenth century—the same social group which cultivated with such devotion the pink and the auricula. Some of the best-known tulip varieties of the eighteen-fifties were raised by an engine-driver near Derby named Tom Storer. And the *Horticultural Magazine* of June 1847 records that a Dulwich florist was so enamoured of his tulips that one frosty night he covered them with blankets taken from his bed, caught cold, and died. This sad story makes perhaps the appropriate contrast—or complement—to one of the many poems on the theme of mortality which have been written about the tulip's rival and Queen. The author is Sir Richard Fanshawe, the date 1648:

> Blown in the morning, thou shalt fade ere noon:
>> What boots a life which in such haste forsakes thee?
> Thou'rt wondrous frolick being to die so soon;
>> And passing proud a little colour makes thee.
>
> If thee thy brittle beauty so deceives,
>> Know then the thing that swells thee is thy bane;
> For the same beauty doth in bloody Leaves
>> The sentence of thy early death contain.
>
> Some clown's coarse lungs will poyson thy sweet flow'r,
>> If by the careless plow thou shalt be torn;
> And many Herods lie in wait each hour
>> To murther thee as soon as thou art born:
>
> Nay, force thy bud to blow; their tyrant breath
> Anticipating life, to hasten Death.

Before we leave the Queen of Flowers we must spare a glance for her lowlier cousin, the wild rose, still one of the loveliest of all flowers, despite the efforts made by florists throughout the centuries to improve on her. This sonnet is by Charles Tennyson Turner:

When Wordsworth found those beds of daffodil
    Beside the lake, a pleasant sight he saw;
I came upon a sweetbriar by a rill,
    In all its summer bloom, without a flaw:
The set of all its flowers my thought recalls,
    And how they took the wind with easy grace;
They rode their arches, shook their coronals,
    And stirr'd their streamers o'er the water's face.
And oh! to watch those azure demoiselles
    Glimpsing about the rosy sprays, that dipt
    Among the weeds,—how daintily equipt
They were! how pure their blue against the pink!
    Light, flitting forms, that haunt our ponds and wells,
Seen, lost and seen, along the reedy brink.

Rosa may be pre-eminently the poet's and the painter's flower, but she cannot claim descent from the Gods, like Iris, of the Oceanides, messenger for Juno and goddess of the rainbow. We quote from Byron:

The moon is up, and yet it is not night;
Sunset divides the sky with her; a sea
Of glory streams along the Alpine height
Of blue Friuli's mountains; Heaven is free
From clouds, but of all colours seems to be,—
Melted to one vast Iris of the West,—
Where the day joins the past Eternity.

This wonderful plant, whose colours the florists have latterly raised to a variety excelling those seen in the rainbow itself, is of great antiquity in cultivation and in art. Some four thousand years ago it was used in the ceremonies and decorations of the Minoans in Crete. Five hundred years later its singular form was displayed in the temple of Tuthmosis III at Karnak. It is the origin of the *fleur-de-lis*, and was the 'yreos' of thirteenth-century English manuscripts.

The purple iris was carried by the Moors in their conquests, both as a living plant and a theme for their decorations. The great Dutch flower paintings, as we have said, seldom omit one of the branching spikes of the bearded iris.

Iris tectorum has been grown on the thatched roof-trees (the name means 'roof iris') of China and Japan for at least a thousand years. Yet curiously enough, the Chinese, though well enough aware of its horticultural and pharmaceutical properties, have not used it in their art. On the contrary, the Japanese have used the flowers of half a dozen kinds in their paintings, and Hiroshige's colour woodcut of the Iris Gardens of Horikiri is one of the outstanding examples of his gift for visual pattern seen from an unusual viewpoint.

One species, *Iris susiana*, the mourning iris, goes back even to the days of myth. Persephone and her handmaidens were picking the flowers when Pluto gathered her to the infernal regions—and, it is said, it was into this iris that the maidens were transformed. This Susian plant belongs to the *Oncocyclus* Irids, most difficult of cultivation, whose rich and sombre glories can only have been matched in prose by Reginald Farrer:

> They are a doomed and lonely race of irreconcilable Troades in weeds of silken crape, sullenly and grandly unresigned to exile and captivity, passing out of their captor's hands in a last defiant blaze of dark and tragic magnificence. They are the chief mourners in their own funeral-pomps, wistful and sombre and royal in an unearthly beauty of their own, native of the Syrian hills that have seen the birth of gods, but strange and hostile to the cruder, colder lands. They are the maidens that went down into hell with Persephone, and yearly in her train they return to make a carpet for her feet across the limestones of the Levant. But not for ours—their loyalty to their mistress holds good only in Syria; they do not recognize her in the rain-cloaks that she wears in the West, and lands of younger divinities shall never twice re-greet such children of mystery as these. And their offspring, the less impossible *Regelio-Cyclus* group, have somehow sold the honour of these silken sad uncertain queens, their mothers, for a mess of comfort in the garden.
>
> One is glad they are such comparatively willing captives, but even their purchased affability one regrets as a betrayal. Nor is it, even in itself, so much to boast of; let them be in deep beds of cow-manure with a foot of hot sand on top; so they will thrive and bloom, but will not for long continue, unless glass and bells be put over them in winter, a set of precautions that turn the garden from a

Hiroshige. The Iris Gardens at Horikiri. 1857. Woodcut in colours.

Lorenzo Lotto (1480–1556). Madonna and Child with St Anthony (detail). 1521.
London, National Gallery.

paradise into a kindergarten or reformatory; and are only permissible when employed to help, as with rare Gentians, but not as the only hopes of prolonging an artificial existence, as with the more fractious Irids of the East.

The lily—and this name meant for some five thousand years the plant we now call the Madonna lily—was one of the earliest of cultivated flowers. The description *candidum*, pure white, now its botanical epithet, was used by Virgil. The flower was represented in the arts of Crete, Assyria, and other civilizations of the eastern Mediterranean. Although the name Madonna lily is a nineteenth-century introduction, Christians have associated the flower with the Virgin Mary since the second century, because, it was said, when her tomb was entered three days after her burial it contained no more than lilies and roses.

When we find the lily named in literature it is usually this kind. Let us turn to one of the comparative newcomers that have enriched our garden floras. William Kerr, whose name is remembered in the *Kerria* of cottage gardens, brought it to the West from Canton as recently as 1804. In the Orient it had been, like some other lilies, grown for the edible bulbs. Why it was called the tiger lily seems unknown: it has been pointed out that it bears little resemblance to any known kind of tiger, though perhaps it may resemble William Blake's creature that burned in the night. The Japanese, it is said, call it the ogre lily, which seems true of the character attributed to the best-known example of the species in literature—which was also so well drawn by John Tenniel. Alice, you will recall,

> came upon a large flower-bed, with a border of daisies, and a willow-tree growing in the middle.
> 'O Tiger-lily,' said Alice, addressing herself to one that was waving gracefully about in the wind, 'I *wish* you could talk!'
> 'We *can* talk,' said the Tiger-lily: 'when there's anybody worth talking to.'
> Alice was so astonished that she couldn't speak for a minute: it quite seemed to take her breath away. At length, as the Tiger-lily only went on waving about, she spoke again, in a timid voice—almost in a whisper. 'And can *all* the flowers talk?'

E

'As well as *you* can,' said the Tiger-lily. 'And a great deal louder.'

'It isn't manners for us to begin, you know,' said the Rose, 'and I really was wondering when you'd speak! Said I to myself, "Her face has got *some* sense in it, though it's not a clever one!" Still, you're the right colour, and that goes a long way.'

'I don't care about the colour,' the Tiger-lily remarked. 'If only her petals curled up a little more, she'd be all right.'

Alice didn't like being criticized, so she began asking questions: 'Aren't you sometimes frightened at being planted out here, with nobody to take care of you?'

'There's the tree in the middle,' said the Rose. 'What else is it good for?'

'But what could it do, if any danger came?' Alice asked.

'It could bark,' said the Rose.

'It says "Bough-wough!" ' cried a Daisy: 'that's why its branches are called boughs!'

'Didn't you know *that*?' cried another Daisy, and here they all began shouting together, till the air seemed quite full of little shrill voices. 'Silence, every one of you!' cried the Tiger-lily, waving itself passionately from side to side, and trembling with excitement. 'They know I can't get at them!' it panted, bending its quivering head towards Alice, 'or they wouldn't dare to do it!'

'Never mind!' Alice said in a soothing tone, and stooping down to the daisies, who were beginning again, she whispered, 'If you don't hold your tongues, I'll pick you!'

There was silence in a moment, and several of the pink daisies turned white.

'That's right!' said the Tiger-lily. 'The daisies are worst of all. When one speaks, they all begin together, and it's enough to make one wither to hear the way they go on!'

Against the ferocious and gaudy tiger-lily we can set by way of contrast the traditional modesty of the lily-of-the-valley, whose lowly stature has inevitably attracted the poets. There is a love poem of 1780 whose author is unknown:

> The fragrant Lily of the Vale,
> So elegantly fair,
> Whose sweets perfume the fanning gale,
> To Chloe I compare.

What tho' on earth it lowly grows
    And strives its head to hide;
Its sweetness far out-vies the rose,
    That flaunts with so much pride.

The costly tulip owes its hue
    To many a gaudy stain;
In this, we view the virgin white
    Of innocence remain.

See how the curious Florist's hand
    Uprears its humble head;
And to preserve the charming flower,
    Transplants it to his bed.

There, while it sheds its sweets around,
    How shines each modest grace!
Enraptur'd how its owner stands,
    To view its lovely face!

But pray, my Chloe, now observe
    The inference of my tale;
May I the Florist be—and thou
    The Lily of the Vale.

The ancient myths, particularly those of Greece, attached to flowers and plants are to most people entertaining, even though few today have had enough of the classics to comprehend more than their merest outlines. To anthropologists they are of significance, throwing, it seems, considerable light on the peculiar habits and beliefs of man. A poet, writer, and thinker like Robert Graves vests them with extraordinary power. Another attitude towards them was that of Alphonse Karr. He was a most learned man whose *Voyage autour de mon Jardin* was much quoted in the last century, that prolific writer on natural history, the Rev J. G. Wood, having made a translation of it in 1854. Whimsical and anecdotal though it is, once started one has difficulty in not reading on, since a totally different attitude from that of the scholar of today is expressed:

The flower of the narcissus was formerly, say the ancient poets, the son of the river Cephisus, who pined away to death from love of his own attractions. Now, I never found the least charm in these fables which force man into everything. I love women under trees, but I don't like them *in* trees, like the hamadryades. All these metamorphoses of men and women into trees and flowers are in my eyes cold and insipid fancies. . . .

With sceptical gusto Karr proceeds to demolish the Narcissus legends. He points out that the Narcissus of the poets is white, with a little exterior yellow and red crown or circle, 'producing a charming effect'. But Virgil, he reminds us, describes the narcissus as red, *pro purpureo Narcisso*, whereas Ovid says it is yellow surrounded with white leaves—not dissimilar to the narcissus we are acquainted with:

> *Croceum florem*
> *Foliis medium cingentibus albis.*

Crowns of narcissus, Karr tells us, were twined in honour of the infernal gods, and placed upon the heads of the dead. He continues:

A sort of fly, very much resembling a drone, burrows in the earth, at a certain period of the year, at the foot of a tuft of narcissus; when, by a subterranean gallery, it has reached the bulb, it deposits an egg in it by means of its wimble; after which it comes out again from the gallery, and resumes its flight. From this egg will issue a worm, which will feed upon the bulb till it shall become a fly similar to that which has just laid it.

I don't know whether the Egyptians were acquainted with this fly, or if they held in sufficient horror so impious an insect, which at the same time eats a god and makes a retreat and asylum of him.

The flies—or at least two species of them—are very much with us today, and their wimbles, which the dictionary tells us are gimlets, continue to lay eggs in the bulbs.

But before the blue-bottle-like Merodon was discovered, and nymphs and shepherds swarmed over England's hills and vales, Daffodil was not a self-admiring boy but a girl—or so at least Michael Drayton had it:

THE DAFFODIL

Batte: Gorbo, as thou cam'st this way
  By yonder little hill,
  Or as thou through the fields didst stray
  Saw'st thou my Daffadil?

  She's in a frocke of Lincolne green,
  Which colour likes her sight,
  And never hath her beautie seene
  But through a vale of white.

  Than roses richer to behold
  That dress up lovers bowres,
  The pansie and the marigold
  Tho Phoebus paramours.

Gorbo: Thou well describ'st the daffadil,
  It is not full an houre
  Since, by the spring, neere yonder hill
  I saw that lovely flowre.

Batte: Yet my faire flowre thou didst not meet,
  Nor newes of her didst bring;
  And yet my Daffadil's more sweet
  Than that by yonder spring.

Gorbo: I saw a shepheard that doth keepe,
  In yonder field of lillies,
  Was making (as he fed his sheepe)
  A wreathe of daffadillies.

Batte: Yet, Gorbo, thou delud'st me still,
  My flowre thou didst not see;
  For, know, my pretty Daffadil
  Is worne of none but mee.

  To show it selfe but neere her seate
  No lilly is so bold,
  Except to shade her from the heate,
  Or keepe her from the cold.

Gorbo: Through yonder vale as I did pass,
        Descending from the hill,
        I met a smerking bonny lass;
        They call her Daffadil:

        Whose presence as along shee went,
        The pretty flowres did greet;
        As though their heads they downeward bent
        With homage to her feet.

        And all the shepherds that were nie,
        From top of every hill,
        Unto the valleyes lowd did crie,
        'There goes sweet Daffadil.'

Batte: Ay, gentle shepheard, now with joy
        Thou all my flocks dost fill;
        That's shee alone, kind shepheards boy,
        Let us to Daffadil.

It is a considerable problem of botanical and poetical history that another spring bulb, now so widely known, and believed to have been established in Britain from early times even by the minority who do not consider it a native, made no appearance in our poetry until mentioned by Thomas Tickell in his poem 'Kensington Garden', published in 1722:

        A flower that first in this sweet garden smil'd
        To virgins sacred, and the Snow-drop styl'd . . .

        Mid frosts and snows triumphant dares appear,
        Mingles the seasons, and leads on the year.

The next reference to the snowdrop in poetry would seem to be by Anthony Whistler (1732–54) in his poem, 'Flowers':

        The Snow-drop first but peeps to light
        And fearful shows its head;
        Their modest merit shines more bright
        By self-distrust misled.

The pansy and the violet have, though quite little things, always attracted the poets. We will quote the mid-eighteenth century William Woty to represent the genus:

> Serene is the morning, the lark leaves his nest,
>   And sings a salute to the dawn.
> The sun with his splendor illumines the East,
>   And brightens the dew on the lawn.
> Whilst the sons of debauch to indulgence give way,
>   And slumber the prime of their hours,
> Let us, my dear Stella! the garden survey,
>   And make our remarks on the flow'rs.
>
> The gay gaudy tulip observe as you walk,
>   How flaunting the gloss of its vest!
> How proud! and how stately it stands on its stalk,
>   In beauty's diversity drest!
> From the rose, the carnation, the pink and the clove,
>   What odours delightfully spring!
> The South wafts a richer perfume to the grove,
>   As he brushes the leaves with his wing.
>
> Apart from the rest, in her purple array,
>   The violet humbly retreats;
> In modest concealment she peeps on the day,
>   Yet none can excel her in sweets:
> So humble, that, tho' with unparallel'd grace
>   She might e'en a palace adorn,
> She oft in the hedge hides her innocent face,
>   And grows at the foot of the thorn.
>
> So Beauty, my fair one! is doubly refin'd,
>   When Modesty heightens her charms,
> When Meekness, like thine, adds a gem to her mind,
>   We long to be lock'd in her arms.
> Though Venus herself from her throne should descend,
>   And the Graces await at her call,
> To thee the gay world would with preference bend,
>   And hail thee the vi'let of all.

The blue of the gentians—or at least some of them—has been written of in excited prose, has seldom been reproduced by the skill of the painter, and has entirely defeated the mechanics of the camera. The kinds now most frequently praised are those growing in the mountains of Europe and Asia. Yet, so far as we know, only three poets have dared to bring the gentian into verse. One was the nineteenth-century American, William Cullen Bryant, writing of the fringed gentian:

> Thou blossom, bright with autumn dew,
> And coloured with the heaven's own blue,
> Thou openest, when the quiet light
> Succeeds the keen and frosty night.
>
> Thou comest not when violets lean
> O'er wandering brooks and springs unseen,
> Or columbines in purple dress'd,
> Nod o'er the ground-bird's hidden nest.
>
> Thou waitest late, and com'st alone,
> When woods are bare and birds are flown,
> And frosts and shortening days portend
> The aged year is near his end.
>
> Then doth thy sweet and quiet eye
> Look through its fringes to the sky,
> Blue—blue—as if that sky let fall
> A flower from its cerulean wall. . . .

Another was that observant naturalist, D. H. Lawrence, who wrote about

> Bavarian gentians, big and dark, only dark
> darkening the day-time torch-like with the smoking
>   blueness of Pluto's gloom,
> ribbed and torch-like, with their blaze of darkness
>   spread blue
> down flattening into points, flattened under the
>   sweep of white day
> torch-flower of the blue-smoking darkness, Pluto's
>   dark-blue daze,

black lamps from the halls of Dio, burning dark blue,
giving off darkness, blue darkness, as Demeter's pale
    lamps give off light,
lead me then, lead me the way.

Reach me a gentian, give me a torch
let me guide myself with the blue, forked torch of
    this flower . . .

Lawrence's obsession with primal darkness reminds us that one of the chief symbolic themes of garden poetry has been the influence of the sun. One encounters it in its simplest symbolism in an anonymous seventeenth-century poem about the marigold. The marigolds, French and African, were early arrivals in the gardens of Europe. They came neither from France nor Africa but, strange to relate, from Mexico. Both were very popular in the seventeenth century.

Down in a garden sate my dearest love,
Her skin more soft and white than down of swan,
More tender-hearted than the Turtle-dove,
    And farre more kind than bleeding Pellican.
I courted her, she rose, and blushing said,
Why was I born to live and die a maid?
With that I pluck a pretty marigold,
Whose dewie leaves shut up when day is done:
Sweeting (I said) arise, look and behold,
A pretty riddle Ile to thee unfold:
These leaves shut in as close as cloyster'd Nun,
Yet will they open when they see the Sun.
    What mean you by this riddle, Sir, she said,
I pray expound it. Then I thus began,
Are not men made for maids, and maids for men?
With that she chang'd her colour and grew wan:
    Since that this riddle you so well unfold,
    Be you the Sun, Ile be the Marigold.

We are so used to the flaunting of another golden flower, the sun-flower, first as the emblem of the Sun King, Louis XIV of France, and more lately in the vibrating colours of Van Gogh, that it is pleasant to observe him in the calmer eighteenth-century vision of Robert Walpole, Earl of Orford:

> Hail! pretty emblem of my fate!
> Sweet flower, you still on Phoebus wait;
> On him you look, and with him move,
> By nature led, and constant love.
>
> Know, pretty flower, that I am he,
> Who are in all so like to thee;
> I, too, my fair one court, and where
> She moves, my eyes I thither steer.
>
> But, yet this difference still I find.
> The sun to you is always kind;
> Does always life and warmth bestow;
> Ah! would my fair one use me so!
>
> Ne'er would I wait till she arose
> From her soft bed and sweet repose;
> But, leaving thee, dull plant by night
> I'd meet my Phillis with delight.

Two other spectacular plants, the rhododendron and the azalea, despite their colours that shame the spectrum and their foliage of infinite variety, have provided but little material for the poet or painter. There is the story told by Xenophon of troops being overcome by honey gathered from the yellow-flowered azalea that grows around the Black Sea. This was touched upon by Tom Moore:

> Ev'n as those bees of Trebizond,—
> Which from the sunniest flowers that clad
> With their pure smile the garden round,
> Draw venom forth that drives men mad . . .

Otherwise, we can only turn to some charming lines by Ralph Waldo Emerson, 'The Rhodora: On Being Asked Whence Is the Flower?' The rhodora, now the botanists' *Rhododendron canadense*, is a reminder that though the most brilliantly coloured rhododendrons in British gardens are Asiatic, the first to arrive were the graceful American species.

In May, when sea-winds pierced our solitudes,
I found the fresh Rhodora in the woods,
Spreading its leafless blooms in a damp nook,
To please the desert and the sluggish brook.
The purple petals, fallen in the pool,
Made the black water with their beauty gay;
Here might the red-bird come his plumes to cool,
And court the flower that cheapens his array.
Rhodora! if the sages ask thee why
This charm is wasted on the earth and sky,
Tell them, dear, that if eyes were made for seeing,
Then Beauty is its own excuse for being:
Why thou wert there, O rival of the Rose!
I never thought to ask, I never knew:
But, in my simple ignorance, suppose
The self-same Power that brought me there brought you.

No collection of poems even remotely connected with flowers could omit some lines by another American poet, Whitman, about another shrub. They occur in his celebrated tribute to President Lincoln:

When lilacs last in the dooryard bloom'd,
And the great star early droop'd in the western sky in the night,
I mourn'd, and yet shall mourn with ever-returning spring.

Ever-returning spring, trinity sure to me you bring,
Lilac blooming perennial and drooping star in the west,
And thought of him I love.

And then, surely, one of the most vivid visual pictures in poetry:

In the dooryard fronting an old farm-house near the white-wash'd
    palings,
Stands the lilac-bush tall-growing with heart-shaped leaves of
    rich green,
With many a pointed blossom rising delicate, with the perfume
    strong I love,
With every leaf a miracle—and from this bush in the dooryard,
With delicate-color'd blossoms and heart-shaped leaves of rich green,
A sprig with its flower I break.

One pauses to reflect on that strange passion for plants which causes man to pursue them and transport them for vast distances. Here is the lilac, first cultivated in European gardens about 300 years before Whitman wrote these words. It had first become widespread in the Old World, and then it had been taken across the Atlantic to the New—where it had already become so common as to be a universally known plant that could here be raised symbolically to great poetic heights.

Man's innate passion for the quest of strange plants has, of course, been responsible for the creation of a feature of the garden upon which we have not yet touched, the greenhouse and conservatory. Here are some lines by William Cowper, written in 1785, when the greenhouse was beginning to evolve from the more aristocratic orangery of the seventeenth and early eighteenth centuries:

> Who loves a garden, loves a green-house too,
> Unconscious of a less propitious clime
> There blooms exotic beauty, warm and snug,
> While the winds whistle and the snows descend.
> The spiry myrtle with unwith'ring leaf
> Shines there and flourishes. The golden boast
> Of Portugal and western India there,
> The ruddier orange and the paler lime,
> Peep through their polish'd foliage at the storm,
> And seem to smile at what they need not fear.
> Th' Amomum there with intermingling flow'rs
> And cherries hangs her twigs. Geranium boasts
> Her crimson honours; and the spangled beau,
> Ficoides, glitters bright the winter long.
> All plants, of ev'ry leaf that can endure
> The winter's frown if screen'd from his shrewd bite,
> Live there and prosper. Those Ausonia claims,
> Levantine regions these; th' Azores send
> Their jessamine, her jessamine remote
> Caffraia: foreigners from many lands,
> They form one social shade, as if convened
> By magic summons of th' Orphean lyre.

Cowper's greenhouse was a mere allotment shack compared with the palaces of glass that Sir Joseph Paxton built at Chatsworth and Decimus

Burton at Kew, for the tropical palms. Not until such existed could the heated, dripping floral world described by W. J. Turner survive away from the tropics:

> I love a still conservatory
>> That's full of giant, breathless palms,
> Azaleas, clematis and vines,
>> Whose quietness great Trees becalms
> Filling the air with foliage,
>> A curved and dreamy statuary . . .

> I love the mossy quietness
>> That grows upon the great stone flags,
> The dark tree-ferns, the staghorn ferns,
>> The prehistoric, antlered stags
> That carven stand and stare among
>> The silent, ferny wilderness . . .

> I like to hear a cold, pure rill
>> Of water trickling low, afar
> With sudden little jerks and purls
>> Into a tank or stoneware jar,
> The song of a tiny sleeping bird
>> Held like a shadow in its trill.

> I watch a white Nyanza float
>> Upon a green, untroubled pool,
> A fairyland Ophelia, she
>> Has cast herself in water cool,
> And lies while fairy cymbals ring
>> Drowned in her fairy castle moat.

> Still as a great jewel is the air
>> With boughs and leaves smooth-carved in it,
> And rocks and trees and giant ferns,
>> And blooms with inner radiance lit,
> And naked water like a nymph
>> That dances tireless, slim and bare.

Silent the Cattleyas blaze
  And thin red orchid shapes of Death
Peer savagely with twisted lips
  Sucking an eerie, phantom breath
With that bright, spotted, fever'd lust
  That watches lonely travellers craze.

Gigantic, mauve and hairy leaves
  Hang like obliterated faces
Full of dim unattained expression
  Such as haunts virgin forest places
When Silence leaps among the trees
  And the echoing heart deceives.

Let us now consider another exotic, the American yucca. For nearly four centuries yuccas have grown in European gardens and yet they still cause comment. They look surprisingly out of place. No other hardy plant grown in our temperate climate has quite the same remarkable form—like a rosette of swords striking into the air. The tall spikes of white, bell-shaped flowers that arise from these dangerous leaves are equally surprising, and few who are not botanically minded will accept that the yucca is related to the lily. It is a plant subject to fashions—enjoyed in the mid-nineteenth century like the aspidistra and the monkey-puzzle, then thrown out of favour, and today much admired again, for it has the 'architectural' attributes now in vogue.

The first kind to be known in England was *Yucca gloriosa*, grown by John Gerard in the reign of Elizabeth I. He had it from a 'learned and skilful apothecary of Excester named Mr Thomas Edwards' who in turn received it from somewhere within 'all the tract of the Indies, from the Magellane Straits unto the Cape of Florida, and in most of the islands of the Canibals, and others adjoining' where it grew naturally. Gerard sent a sucker of it to France for Robin, the royal gardener.

A distinguished English Victorian gardener, Henry Bright, wrote delightfully of the shrub:

> Not long ago I was at a stately place in Shropshire, and at the end of
> a broad walk, where a circle of yuccas had been planted, there were

no less than five in full flower, throwing up pale jets of blossom, like fountains, towards the sky. I never saw anything more perfect in its way. But it is said that the right time to see a yucca is by moonlight. There is a very striking passage in one of the letters of the most remarkable of American women, Margaret Fuller (afterwards Countess D'Ossoli), in which she says:

'This flower' (it was the *Yucca filamentosa*) 'was made for the moon as the Heliotrope is for the sun, and refuses other influences, or to display her beauty in any other light. Many white flowers are far more beautiful by day. The lily, for instance, needs the broadest light to manifest its purity, but these transparent leaves of greenish white, which look dull in the day, are melted by the moon to glistening silver. . . .'

The second evening I went out into the garden again. In clearest moonlight stood my flower, more beautiful than ever. The stalk pierced the air like a spear; all the little bells had erected themselves around it in a most graceful array, with petals more transparent than silver, and of softer light than the diamond. Their edges were clearly but not sharply defined—they seemed to have been made by the moon's rays. The leaves, which had looked ragged by day, now seemed fringed by most delicate gossamer, and the plant might claim, with pride, its distinctive epithet of *filamentosa*.

Probably the most famous 'flower of night' is the night-blowing cereus, which was the subject of one of the best-known illustrations in Dr Thornton's *Temple of Flora*—gold, white, and ghostly in the moonlight, with the hands on the church clock in the background standing at three minutes past midnight. On this characteristic symbol of the Romantic Movement Felicia Dorothea Hemans wrote a superb romantic poem:

> Children of night! unfolding meekly, slowly
> To the sweet breathings of the shadowy hours,
> When dark blue heavens look softest and most holy,
> And glow-worm light is in the forest bowers;
>   To solemn things and deep,
>   To spirit-haunted sleep,
>   To thoughts, all purified
> From earth, ye seem allied;
>   O dedicated flowers!

Ye, from the gaze of crowds your beauty veiling,
Keep in dim vestal urns the sweetness shrined;
Till the mild moon, on high serenely sailing,
Looks on you tenderly and sadly kind.
    So doth love's dreaming heart
    Dwell from the throng apart,
    And but to shades disclose
    The inmost thought which glows
        With its pure heart entwined.

Shut from the sounds wherein the day rejoices,
To no triumphant song your petals thrill,
But send forth odours with the faint, soft voices
Rising from hidden streams, when all is still.
    So doth lone prayer arise,
    Mingling with secret sighs,
    When grief unfolds, like you,
    Her breast, for heavenly dew
        In silent hours to fill.

The subject of this poem is, as we say, famous as much for the manner of its illustration—'the flower by Reinagle, moonlight by Pether'—as for its description by the poet. This illustration—like others in *The Temple of Flora*—combines a romantic treatment with botanical accuracy.

In Italy such flower studies as those of Pisanello in the fifteenth century, and the lilies and other details associated with early paintings of the Madonna, would qualify as perfectly understood botanical representations, though they were, one might say, by-products of the artist's concern with wider matters. The French Books of Hours of the sixteenth century contain, again as a decorative side-line, exquisitely true plant drawings. At certain periods church sculpture was representative, and in England the 'leaves of Southwell' of the late thirteenth century are extraordinarily life-like compared with all but a tiny proportion of British graphic art, such as the detail in the Wilton diptych of a century later.

The first life-like representations on any scale in England are found not in pictures but in carvings, the astonishing decorative wood-work of Grinling Gibbons and his school. This coincides with the tentative bota-

Grinling Gibbons. Flowers. Carving in wood. *Country Life* photograph.
National Trust : Petworth House, Sussex.

John James Audubon. Lesser Redpoll on *Symphoricarpus Racemosus* (Snowberry).
From *The Birds of America*. 1837. *London, British Museum.*

nical studies of Alexander Marshal of about the same period. Not for several decades did English graphic botanical artistry achieve the quality displayed with such profusion by Gibbons in his lime wood.

In North America some of the earliest and still some of the most interesting botanical figures are found as subsidiary subjects in the masterly bird portraits of J. J. Audubon. For instance, his lovely plate of the Lesser Redpoll among sprays of the snowberry—the *Symphoricarpus* (which means a plant bearing clustered fruit) of the botanists—was made when this plant was still little known in the Old World. Soon it was to become so widely spread that in the British Flora today it is cited as naturalized. It was first cultivated, no doubt, for the glistening berries. The flowers are tiny, though visited by hundreds of bumble-bees after what must be almost microscopic drops of nectar. Very soon, however, sportsmen discovered that pheasants liked the fruits, which have a quality that is now equally appreciated by flower arrangers: they keep fresh, white, and plump long after other berries begin to decay.

All over the world, and since ancient times, flowers and garlands have been an essential of celebrations. One example of many is the flower feast at Genzano in Italy which was described by Hans Christian Andersen in 1830:

How shall I describe the first glance into the street—that bright picture as I then saw it? The entire, long, gently ascending street was covered over with flowers; the ground colour was blue: it looked as if they had robbed all the gardens, all the fields to collect flowers enough of the same colour to cover the street; over these lay in long stripes, green, composed of leaves, alternately with rose-colour; at some distance from this was a similar stripe, and between this a layer of dark red flowers, so as to form, as it were, a broad border to the whole carpet. The middle of this represented stars and suns, which were formed by a close mass of yellow, round, and star-like flowers; more labour still had been spent upon the formation of names—here flower was laid upon flower, leaf upon leaf. The whole was a living flower-carpet, a mosaic floor, richer in pomp of colouring than any thing which Pompeii can shew. Not a breath of air stirred—the flowers lay immovable, as if they were heavy, firmly set precious stones.

From all windows were hung upon the walls large carpets, worked in leaves and flowers, representing holy pictures. Here Joseph led the ass on which sat the Madonna and the child; roses formed the faces, the feet, and the arms; gilly-flowers and anemones their fluttering garments; and crowns were made of white water-lilies, brought from Lake Nemi. Saint Michael fought with the dragon; the holy Rosalia showered down roses upon the dark blue globe; wherever my eye fell flowers related to the biblical legends, and the people all round about were as joyful as myself.

The use of flowers as emblems of human mortality is very old. This was exemplified in antiquity by the making of Adonis gardens. A vase was filled with short-lived plants which were contrasted with the immortality of the bay. The tradition lived on into medieval times and is even represented on tombs. It died out, or at the best became distorted, in the days of the Renaissance.

In the seventeenth century Robert Herrick plucked a whole array of flowers from the garden to point out the impermanence of human love and life in 'A Meditation for His Mistress':

> You are a Tulip seen to day,
> But (Dearest) of so short a stay;
> That where you grew, scarce man can say.
>
> You are a lovely July-flower,
> Yet one rude wind, or ruffling shower,
> Will force you hence (and in an houre).
>
> You are a sparkling Rose i' th' bud,
> Yet lost, ere that chast flesh and blood
> Can show where you or grew, or stood.
>
> You are a full-spread, faire-set Vine,
> And can with Tendrills love intwine,
> Yet dry'd, ere you distil your Wine.
>
> You are like Balme inclosèd (well)
> In Amber, or some Crystall shell,
> Yet lost ere you transfuse your smell.

You are a dainty Violet,
Yet wither'd, ere you can be set
Within the Virgin's Coronet.

You are the Queen all flowers among:
But die you must (faire Maid) ere long,
As He, the maker of this Song.

Surely, however, the most perfect lines on the fugitive nature of flowers and man are those of another seventeenth-century parson, George Herbert:

I made a posy, while the day ranne by:
Here will I smell my remnant out, and ty
    My life within this band.
But Time did becken to the flowres, and they
By Noone most cunningly did steale away,
    And wither'd in my hand.

My hand was next to them, and then my heart:
I tooke without more thinking in good part
    Time's gentle admonition;
Who did so sweetly death's sad tast convey,
Making my mind to smell my fatall day,
    Yet sugring the suspicion.

Farewell deare flowres, sweetly your time ye spent,
Fitt, while ye liv'd, for smell or ornament,
    And after death for cures:
I follow strait, without complaints or greif,
Since if my scent be good, I care not if
    It be as short as yours.

4

Fruits of the Earth

Eve, smiling, pluck'd the apple, then
Laugh'd, sigh'd—and tasted it again:
'Strange such a pleasant, juicy thing
On a forbidden tree should spring!'

But had she seen with clearer eyes,
Or had the serpent been less wise,
She'd scarce have shown such little wit
As to let Adam taste of it!

Lady Margaret Sackville's wisdom, many thousands of years too late to be of the least use, at least throws some light on human nature and, as it is regarded in much of the world, the fruit of fruits. In England the apple was long taken for granted, and the early pomologists pay greater attention to pears and the more tender fruit. This was not the way of the poet John Philips, who, bristling with patriotism, regarded the apple as his country's finest fruit, and cyder its proper drink. All this he put in his poem, *Cyder*, in 1709. And lovely were the names of the old fruit:

The *Pippin* burnish'd o'er with Gold, the *Moile*
Of sweetest hony'd Taste, the fair *Permain*,
Temper'd, like comliest Nymph, with red and white.
Salopian Acres flourish with a Growth
Peculiar, styl'd the *Ottley*: Be thou first
This Apple to transplant; if to the Name
It's Merit answers, no where shalt thou find
A Wine more priz'd, or laudable of Taste.
Nor does the *Eliot* least deserve thy Care,
Nor *John-Apple*, whose wither'd Rind, entrencht
With many a Furrow, aptly represents

Attributed to Cornelis de Heem. Fruit and Flowers. 1662.
London, Victoria and Albert Museum.

Marc Meucci, of Florence. Apples and Grapes. c. 1860. *London, Paul Larsen.*

Decrepid Age: nor that from *Harvey* nam'd
Quick-relishing: Why should we sing the *Thrift*,
Codling, or *Pomroy*, or of pimpled Coat
The *Russet*, or the *Cat's Head's* weighty Orb
Enormous in its Growth: for various Use
Tho' these are meet, tho' after full repast
Are oft requir'd, and crown the rich Desert?

  What, tho' the *Pear-Tree* rival not the Worth
Of Ariconian Products? Yet her Freight
Is not contemn'd, yet her wide-branching Arms
Best screen thy Mansion from the fervent Dog
Adverse to Life; the wintry Hurricanes
In vain imploy their Roar, her Trunc unmov'd
Breaks the strong Onset, and controls their Rage.
Chiefly the *Bosbury*, whose large Increase,
Annual, in sumptuous Banquets claims Applause.
Thrice acceptable Bev'rage! could but Art
Subdue the floating Lee, *Pomona's* self
Would dread thy Praise, and shun the dubious Strife.
Be it thy choice, when Summer-Heats annoy,
To sit beneath her leafy Canopy,
Quaffing rich Liquids: Oh! how sweet t' enjoy
At once her Fruits, and hospitable Shade!

  But how with equal number shall we match
The *Musk's* surpassing Worth! that earliest gives
Sure hopes of racy Wine, and in its Youth
Its tender Nonage, loads the spreading Boughs
With large and juicy Off-spring, that defies
The Vernal Nippings, and cold Syderal Blasts!
Yet let her to the *Red-Streak* yield, that once
Was of the Sylvan Kind, unciviliz'd,
Of no Regard, 'till Scudamore's skilful Hand
Improv'd her, and by courtly Discipline
Taught her the savage Nature to forget:
Hence styl'd the *Scudamorean* Plant; whose Wine
Who-ever tastes, let him with grateful Heart
Respect that ancient loyal House, and wish
The noble Peer, that now transcends our Hopes
In early Worth, his Country's justest Pride,
Uninterrupted Joy, and Health entire.

> Let every Tree in every Garden own
> The *Red-streak* as supream; whose pulpous Fruit
> With Gold irradiate, and Vermilian shines
> Tempting, not fatal, as the Birth of that
> Primaeval interdicted Plant, that won
> Fond Eve in hapless Hour to taste, and die.
> This, of more bounteous Influence, inspires
> Poetic Raptures, and the lowly Muse
> Kindles to loftier Strains; even I perceive
> Her sacred Virtue. See! the Numbers flow
> Easie, whilst, chear'd with her nectareous Juice,
> Hers, and my Country's Praises I exalt.

The 'numbers flowed' so 'easie' that John Philips staked his claim to be for all time the Laureate of the Orchard. *Cyder* runs to some fifteen hundred lines of tight-packed informative verse. Poets of our own day have dared to tackle the same theme only in lyric quantities—but none more evocatively than Laurie Lee:

> Behold the apples' rounded worlds:
> juice-green of July rain,
> the black polestar of flower, the rind
> mapped with its crimson stain.
>
> The russet, crab and cottage red
> burn to the sun's hot brass,
> then drop like sweat from every branch
> and bubble in the grass.
>
> They lie as wanton as they fall,
> and where they fall and break,
> the stallion clamps his crunching jaws,
> the starling stabs his beak.
>
> In each plump gourd the cidery bite
> of boys' teeth tears the skin;
> the waltzing wasp consumes his share,
> the bent worm enters in.

❖◇❖◇❖◇❖◇❖◇❖◇❖◇❖◇❖◇❖◇❖◇❖◇❖◇❖◇❖◇❖◇❖◇❖◇❖◇❖

I, with as easy hunger, take
entire my season's dole;
welcome the ripe, the sweet, the sour,
the hollow and the whole.

An unusual treatment of the symbolism of the apple is to be found in a poem by that now neglected author of the nineties, John Davidson:

Their mystery none discovers,
So none can tell—
Not the most passionate lovers
Of garth and fell;
For the silent sunlight weaves
The orchard spell,
Bough, bole and root,
Mysterious, hung with leaves,
Embossed with fruit.
Though merle and throstle were loud,
Silent *their* passion in spring,
A blush of blossom wild-scented;
And now when no song-birds sing,
They are heavy with apples and proud
And supremely contented—
All fertile and green and sappy,
No wish denied,
Exceedingly quiet and happy
And satisfied!

No jealousy, anger, or fashion
Of strife
Perturbs in their stations
The apple-trees. Life
Is an effortless passion,
Fruit, bough and stem,
A beautiful patience
For them.
Frost of the harvest-moon
Changes their sap to wine:
Ruddy and golden soon
Their clustered orbs will shine,

By favour
Of many a wind,
Of morn and noon and night,
Fulfilled from core to rind
With savour
Of all delight.

The harvesting of apples holds, for any owner of an orchard, something of the same symbolic significance as the corn harvest of the farmer. Its emotional undertones have been transcribed with exquisite precision by Robert Frost:

My long two-pointed ladder's sticking through a tree
Toward heaven still,
And there's a barrel that I didn't fill
Beside it, and there may be two or three
Apples I didn't pick upon some bough.
But I am done with apple-picking now.
Essence of winter sleep is on the night,
The scent of apples: I am drowsing off.
I cannot rub the strangeness from my sight
I got from looking through a pane of glass
I skimmed this morning from the drinking trough
And held against the world of hoary grass.
It melted, and I let it fall and break.
But I was well
Upon my way to sleep before it fell,
And I could tell
What form my dreaming was about to take.
Magnified apples appear and disappear,
Stem end and blossom end,
And every fleck of russet showing clear.
My instep arch not only keeps the ache,
It keeps the pressure of a ladder-round.
I feel the ladder sway as the boughs bend.
And I keep hearing from the cellar bin
The rumbling sound
Of load on load of apples coming in.
For I have had too much
Of apple-picking: I am overtired

Of the great harvest I myself desired.
There were ten thousand thousand fruit to touch,
Cherish in hand, lift down, and not let fall.
For all
That struck the earth,
No matter if not bruised or spiked with stubble,
Went sure to the cider-apple heap
As of no worth.
One can see what will trouble
This sleep of mine, whatever sleep it is.
Were he not gone,
The woodchuck could say whether it's like his
Long sleep, as I describe its coming on,
Or just some human sleep.

Presumably because of its pristine association with the Garden of Eden the apple has always received more attention from writers than any other fruit. Let us now, by way of contrast, consider a poor and nowadays neglected relation. The quotation is from *Flora and Sylva*, 1904:

Apart from its fruit, the beauty of an old Quince tree makes it worth a place in my garden, with its sweeping pendulous branches, knotted and gnarled grotesquely, distinct in their dark colour, and quite unlike the ordinary fruit tree in effect. The large cup-shaped flowers of white or flesh pink are beautiful, hanging like single Roses from the tips of every side shoot among the soft rounded leaves, silvery white beneath. And when in Autumn the boughs hang yet lower beneath their load of fruits, whose colour outvies the golden leaves, few trees grown for effect are finer than this 'golden apple of Hesperides'. . . .

The beauty of the old Quince orchards of southern Europe, where the fruits hang until fully mellowed, explains the estimation in which it was held by classic writers, for whom the Quince stood as an emblem of love and happiness, dedicated to Venus and used in the adornment of her temples. Its fruits were fabled as the forbidden fruit of scripture, were worshipped by the Greeks, and for ages played a part in marriage rites, a custom maintained in our own country as late as 1725. Travellers tell of Chinese Quinces which are tender and delicious eaten raw, but the Quince of Europe is not good until cooked.

For ages Quince jelly and marmalade have been famed, and were long the only kinds known. The fruits are far richer in flavour than most cooking Pears, stewed in the same way and served hot with sugar, and cream or butter, or when cold if so preferred; again, for an added zest to Apple tarts the Quince is most useful in countries like our own, where the Apple is the great winter fruit. Even when the ripe fruits (which do not keep long) are gone, a reserve of syrup will supply their flavour.

Apart from the peach, the fruit which is generally esteemed above others for sheer *flavour* is, with little doubt, the strawberry. 'Only the Rheumatic,' wrote E. A. Bunyard, 'regards the strawberry with a jaundiced eye; for the rest it is the very primrose of fruits, announcing the season has opened again, sounding the death knell to oranges and bananas, which perforce, have sustained us since our last apples and pears came to an untimely end.' It is the fruit that was evolved in England out of species from Virginia and Chile at the beginning of the last century, and was at first known as the English strawberry. Yet centuries before that the tiny fruit of the wild strawberry was esteemed so greatly that there are records of Henry VIII's gardeners going into the woods to collect roots. And it was of the same fruit that William Butler (who was born in Henry's reign) said—according to Isaac Walton—'Doubtless God could have made a better berry, but doubtless God never did.' The plant has other qualities, such as the 'leaves dying, which yield a most excellent cordial smell' to which we shall refer later. Then there is the heraldic significance. Here is Dame Edith Sitwell's tribute:

> Beneath my dog-furred leaves you see
> The creeping strawberry
> In a gold net
> The footprints of the dew have made more wet.

> Mahomet resting on a cloud of gold
> Dreamed of the strawberry
> Made of the purpling gauzy heat
> And jasper dust trod by his golden feet.—

The jasper dust beside
The fountain tide,
The water jacynth-cold,
The water-ripples like mosaics gold
Have made my green leaves wide and water-cold.

From palaces among the widest leaves
My Sun, my Fatima,
Shows her gold face and sighs,
And darkness dies.

At noon my Fatima, my bright gazelle,
Walks by each gauzy bell
Of strawberries made of such purpling air
As the heat knows, and there

When Fatima, my dew with golden foot,
Comes like all the music of the air
Then shine my berries till those golden footsteps die—
Like all the glittering desert of the air when the
       hot sun goes by.

Another fruit of the 'hot sun' which has an aesthetic, if not a strictly literary connotation is the pineapple. Many are the stone finials apparently in its image which decorate garden walls, gate piers, and the cornices of eighteenth- and early nineteenth-century buildings. If we turn to the works of Bartholomaeus, one of the first English naturalists, we read that

> Pinea, the Pine apple, is the fruit of the Pine tree, as Pliny sayeth. And is great and round by the stalks, and sharp at the ende, and first greene, and more full when it is ripe, with colour as it were the colour of a Castane. The pine apple is the most greatest nut, and conceiveth in itself instead of fruite many kernels, closed in full hard shales.

The true pine-apple was, therefore, the cone of *Pinus pinea*, the stone pine, 'artist's model, and the conspicuous feature of the foreground in many a Turner and Claude landscape'. The 'many kernels' were the large edible seeds, the *pignons* of today. These the Roman conquerors carried about with them. Remains of cones and seeds have been found as far north as England (but never, it seems, traces of the wood—showing that the tree was not grown here). Yet the *pignons* that the Romans brought with them were not for eating, but for altar fuel. More surprisingly, at Witcombe near Gloucester was found a crude terra-cotta fir-cone—which if today used as a finial we should call a pine-apple.

The answer to this problem seems to be that the stone-pine pine-apple was an emblem of fertility in the cult of Mithras, and as such was modelled or carved. Even when that cult died out, there was something aesthetically satisfying about its form that caused it to be used down to medieval times. And when, in the seventeenth century, the similarity of form of the pine-cone and the newly found fruit was observed, so that the name was transferred and its new use became general, the same strange feeling for its shape caused craftsmen to adapt it purely as a decoration, with the addition of the basal leaves of *Ananas* elaborated into an acanthus-like growth. Or are we quite wrong, and are our pine-apple ornaments no more than formal decorations descended from the stone-pine cone which, with the change in meaning of the word pine-apple, we misapprehend?

In Europe the great age of pineapple culture was the mid-nineteenth century. The aristocracy and plutocracy with their rapidly improving pineries vied with one another to produce larger and heavier fruit. There was exhibited in 1848 a picture at the Royal Academy which, the newspapers said, attracted great attention. It was described as an almost matchless assemblage of magnificent fruit. 'The principal object in the composition, whether considered as to size, weight, form or colour, was a stupendous pineapple weighing 16 lbs. and 19 inches long.' This assemblage was grown at Blenheim Palace. So greatly did it please the Duke of Marlborough that he sent the artist, George Lance, a cheque for two hundred guineas.

A painting which is perhaps more to modern taste, and is certainly one of the earliest portraits of the fruit, is the delightful conversation piece which is believed to depict Charles II (who it undoubtedly is) being presented with the first fruit to be grown in England by his gardener Rose (of whom no portrait or description is known). The scene has been identified with several gardens, notably at Ham House and Dorney. Architecturally, the buildings bear no resemblance to those houses, and all the evidence indicates that they were in Holland, where the king

Henry Danckerts. 'The Pineapple Picture'. *The Marchioness of Cholmondeley.*

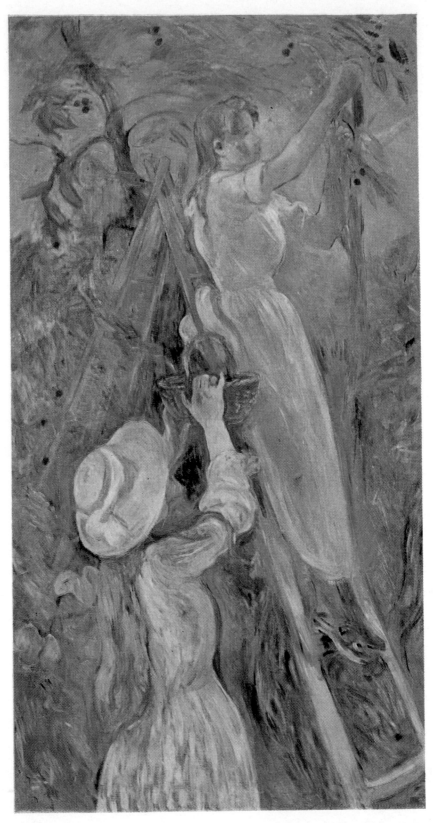

Berthe Morisot. The Cherry-Picker. 1891. *Madame Ernest Rouart.*

stayed during his absence from England. Further, though the pineapple was consumed in England by Oliver Cromwell, there is no evidence of its cultivation in England before the early eighteenth century.

J. C. Loudon in his great book of 1838 on trees wrote that 'the cherry has always been a favourite tree with poets; the brilliant red of the fruit, the whiteness and profusion of the blossoms, and the vigorous growth of the tree, affording abundant similes: but the instances where they occur are too numerous, and too well known, to be suitable for quotation'. He tells us instead that in 1828 he travelled for several days through one continuous avenue of cherry trees, from Strasburg by a circuitous route to Munich. He tells us, too, of the Feast of Cherries at Hamburg, when children parade the street with green boughs, ornamented with cherries. The custom arose in 1432 when the city of Hamburg was besieged by the Hussites. One of the citizens named Wolf proposed that all the children in the city, between seven and fourteen years of age, should be clad in mourning, and sent as suppliants to the enemy. Procopius Nasus, chief of the Hussites, was so much moved by this spectacle that he not only promised to spare the city, but regaled the young suppliants with cherries and other fruits; and the children returned crowned with leaves, shouting 'Victory!', and holding boughs laden with cherries in their hands.

The story goes that Lucullus brought the cherry to Europe in about 68 B.C. from Cerasus (now Giresun) which he destroyed along with the Kingdom of Pontus and King Mithridates.

The cultivation of cherries in Kent is of considerable antiquity: they were brought by boat and sold in London at least five hundred years ago. The old cherry-seller's cry has been the theme of well-known songs. Here is Herrick's version:

> Cherrie-ripe, Ripe, Ripe, I cry,
> Full and faire ones; come and buy:
> If so be, you ask me where
> They doe grow, I answer: There,
> Where my Julia's lips doe smile;
> There's the Land, or Cherry-Ile:
> Whose Plantations fully show
> All the yeere, where Cherries grow

So far as we know, a feeling shared by most gardeners was first publicly expressed by Joseph Addison in 1712: 'I value my garden more for being full of blackbirds than of cherries, and very frankly give them fruit for their songs.' The word *avium*, meaning 'of birds', is the botanical name of the ancestor of most of the large-fruited cherries, and refers to the passion that birds have for the fruit.

Since Loudon's day a whole new world of cherries has come to the West, particularly the United States, where they have been extensively studied and planted. In spite of Housman's

> Loveliest of trees, the cherry now
> Is hung with bloom along the bough...

these oriental kinds are commonly known as the flowering or ornamental cherries—merely because they are for display and not for eating, the fruit being small and worthless. Aesthetically, however, the cherries that the Japanese have developed from Chinese species are important: the charming names, such as Jo-nioi, 'supreme fragrance,' Tai Haku, 'the great white cherry,' Shirofugen, 'the great white god,' and Amanogowa, 'the milky way,' suggest the poetry that surrounds these trees.

Collingwood Ingram has described how the cherry is deeply involved in the mythology and history of Japan, the incidents that occurred being displayed in varying forms of art. One of the most frequently illustrated anecdotes concerns the ingenuity of the warrior-general Kojima. His Emperor, Go-Daigo, had the misfortune to fall into the hands of enemies who, to save further trouble, were taking him to exile on the island of Kyushu. Kojima had already escaped. Knowing the road which the Emperor's captors would follow, he moved forward speedily and secretly to an inn where they would halt. Beside it grew a very famous cherry tree, then at the season of full flower. The Emperor knew and admired this tree. Kojima felt certain that he would pause, see, and admire its loveliness. So he tore back a strip of bark and on the surface underneath he wrote a message of encouragement to Go-Daigo.

The story of the discovery of the winter-flowering cherry, Jugatsu Sakura (the name means autumn cherry) goes back to A.D. 408. One mild November day the Emperor Richu was enjoying himself in his garden when a cherry petal drifted over and fell in his drink, which was rice spirit. At first he thought that this was a vision inspired by the spirit, but after being reassured that it was a reality, he ordered a search to be made for its source that was to continue until it was found. Finally the single tree was run to earth in a neighbouring suburb. Since then it has spread to many thousands of Western gardens.

In the Far East one of the most esteemed delicacies among fruits has always been the lychee. This is borne upon a tree whose form is rather like that of a small chestnut, though the leaves resemble those of the laurel. The tree blooms in May, and the rose-red fruit, which ripens in July, has soft white flesh surrounding a dark brown stone. So tender is the flesh, and so fragrant the taste, that many Chinese poets have written of the lychee, and many artists have depicted it.

The Emperor Hsuan Tsung, who reigned in the eighth century, ordered a regular supply of lychees to be sent from Szechuan in southern China to his court in the north for the delectation of the famous beauty, Yang Kuei-fei, who was born in Szechuan and had developed a taste for lychees in her childhood. The fruits had to be conveyed on horseback for a thousand miles, over rough roads, and delivered to the Emperor's favourite in less than seven days.

Long before that, in A.D. 120, the poet Wang I had celebrated the excellencies of the fruit in this poem (the translation is Arthur Waley's):

> Sombre as the heavens when morning clouds arise,
> Bushy as a great broom held across the sky,
> Vast as the spaces of a lofty house,
> Deep fretted as a line of stony hills.
> Long branches twining,
> Green leaves clustering.
> And all a-glimmer like a mist that lightly lies
> Across the morning sun;
> All spangled, darted with fire like a sky
> Of populous stars.
> Shell like a fisherman's red net;
> Fruit white and lustrous as a pearl . . .
> Lambent as the jewel of Ho, more strange
> Than the saffron-stone of Hsia.

> Now sigh we at the beauty of its show,
> Now triumph in its taste.
> Sweet juices lie in the mouth,
> Soft scents invade the mind.
> All flavours here are joined, yet none is master;
> A hundred diverse tastes
> Blend in such harmony no man can say
> That one outstrips the rest. Sovereign of sweets,
> Peerless, pre-eminent fruit, who dwellest apart
> In noble solitude!

Apart from the apple and the cherry, the English poets have, surprisingly, had little to say of any of the other Western fruits that flourished so memorably in Andrew Marvell's seventeenth-century garden:

> What wond'rous Life in this I lead!
> Ripe Apples drop about my head;
> The Luscious Clusters of the Vine
> Upon my Mouth do crush their Wine;
> The Nectaren and curious Peach
> Into my hands themselves do reach;
> Stumbling on Melons, as I pass,
> Insnar'd with Flow'rs, I fall on Grass...

There is, indeed, a certain poetry in the mere names of the varieties of peach growing on the walls of a garden in the mid-eighteenth century: Old Newington, Albermarle, Minion, Belle Chevereuse, Rumbullion, Noblisse, Montaubano, Red Magdalen and Nevite (the spellings are as the gardener wrote them). And there was certainly a poetic impulse in the mind of the seventeenth-century nurseryman Leonard Gurle of White Chapel who, on raising a supreme nectarine, found a name for it by turning his own bucolic surname back to front—Elruge.

And a contemporary of Marvell's, a little-known metaphysical poet named Richard Leigh, published in 1675 a love poem based upon a charming analogy between the peach and a lady who, in the colloquial English of the nineteen-twenties, would also have been referred to as a 'peach'.

Unknown Chinese Artist of the Ming Dynasty. Lychees.
Detail of a scroll painting on silk. *London, British Museum.*

Paul Van Somer. Elizabeth, Lady Tanfield. c. 1600. *Group-Captain Loel Guinness.*

Behold, wherever she does pass,
  How all the am'rous Trees contend,
Whose loaded Arms should her embrace,
  While with their fruit tow'rds her they bend;
    As if the willing Branches meant,
    To her, their Bounty to present.

The upper Boughs all bending low,
  Her raisëd Arm seem to prevent;
While those, that level with her grow,
  To meet her easie hand consent.
      To court her thus, Lo, ev'ry Peach
      Submits it self, within her reach.

These she prefers, refusing those,
  Unhappy, in their rip'ning last;
Persuaded by her Eye to choose,
  As that, the colour'd fruit does tast;
      Which her Desire does gently move
      To what her Sense did first approve.

Fair, as this golden Fruit here seems,
  The Sun, with kind Salutes thus streaks,
And gilding them with am'rous Beams,
  Prints purple Kisses on their Cheeks:
      Kisses soft as that tender Down,
      Which their yong blushing Cheeks does crown.

Ah! could the fair, who this does see,
  Be by this great Example won,
And learn but thus to smile on me,
  As they smile on the kissing Sun.
      Bright as their Cheeks with Kisses shine,
      Hers brighter should appear with *mine*.

It is odd how little that other orchard tree, the walnut, has been celebrated by the poets, considering that the ancient Latin name, *Juglans*,
means no less than Jove's nut. Possibly the greatest contribution it makes
to our delights is the furniture carved from the timber. The nuts were

G

scattered at Greek and Roman weddings—because, the walnut being dedicated to Diana, the bride was deserting the ranks of that goddess for those of Hymen, the rose-and-marjoram-decorated god of marriage. In Limerick the exquisite gloves the people made could be placed within a walnut shell. In parts of Europe the walnut and the oak were supposed never to grow together, and the walnut was also held to be a witch's tree.

The black walnut of North America is grown in Europe as a more beautiful tree than the common kind; the timber is also of superb quality. The nut has not the same attraction to the human palate, but the Old and the New World kinds are equally favoured by squirrels and crows: in Britain they usually consume the entire crop. Audubon's superb illustration of the American Crow shows him perched in a black walnut tree.

Abraham Cowley is, we believe, the only poet to treat, in his *Plantarum Libri*, of this tree and enumerate its properties as they were in the seventeenth century. He describes the brain-like formation of the fruit delightfully:

> The Walnut then approach'd, more large and tall,
> His fruit, which we a Nut, the gods an Acorn, call:
> Jove's Acorn, which does no small praise confess,
> To've call'd it Man's Ambrosia had been less.
> Nor can this head-like Nut, shap'd like the brain,
> Within, be said that form by change to gain,
> Or Caryon* call'd by learned Greeks in vain:
> For membranes, soft as silk, her kernels bind,
> Whereof the inmost is of tend'rest kind,
> Like those which on the brain of man we find;
> All which are in a seam-join'd shell enclos'd,
> Which of this brain the skull may be suppos'd.
> This very skull envelop'd is again
> In a green coat, her pericranium.
> Lastly, that no objection may remain,
> To thwart her near alliance to the brain,
> She nourishes the hair, rememb'ring how
> Herself deform'd without her leaves does show
> On barren scalps she makes fresh honours grow.

* Caryon was the Greek name for the walnut—now applied, as *Carya*, to the pecan and other nuts.

Her timber is for various uses good;
The carver she supplies with lasting wood.
She makes the painter's fading colours last;
A table she affords us, and repast;
E'en while we feast, her oil our lamp supplies;
The rankest poison by her virtue dies,
The mad dog's foam, and taint of raging skies.
The Pontic king,* who liv'd where poisons grew,
Skilful in antidotes, her virtues knew.
Yet envious Fates, that still with merit strive,
And man, ungrateful from the orchard drive
This sov'reign Plant excluded from the field,
Unless some useless nook a station yield,
Defenceless in the common road she stands,
Expos'd to restless war of vulgar hands;
By neighb'ring clowns, and passing rabble torn,
Batter'd with stones by boys, and left forlorn.

We refer elsewhere to the splendour of Salvator's chestnut—the so-called Spanish chestnut—and we may now mention its fruit. That was also famous in classical times when Virgil (translated by Dryden) wrote:

My self will search our planted Grounds at home,
For downy Peaches and the glossy Plum;
And thrash the Chesnuts in the Neighb'ring Grove,
Such as my Amarillis us'd to love.

Milton, too:

While hisses on my hearth the pulpy pear,
And black'ning chestnuts start and crackle there.

The American chestnut is quite distinct from the tree of classical repute. It is now tragically devastated by a disease imported from Asia against which it carries no defence. It was of the fruit of this, though equally true of the other kind, that Emily Dickinson queried:

* Mithridates.

How fits his Umber Coat
The Tailor of the Nut?
Combined without a seam
Like Raiment of a Dream—

Who spun the Auburn Cloth?
Computed how the girth?
The Chestnut aged grows
In those primeval Clothes—

We know that we are wise—
Accomplished in Surprise—
Yet by this Countryman—
This nature—how undone!

As a reminder of the days before *Endothia parasitica* obliterated tens of thousands of acres of American chestnut, we reprint a passage from that philosopher of an idealized nature, Henry Thoreau:

When chestnuts were ripe I laid up half a bushel for winter. It was very exciting at that season to roam the then boundless chestnut woods of Lincoln—they now sleep their long sleep under the railroad—with a bag on my shoulder, and a stick to open burrs with in my hand, for I did not always wait for the frost, amid the rustling of leaves and the loud reproofs of the red-squirrels and the jays, whose half-consumed nuts I sometimes stole, for the burrs they had selected were sure to contain sound ones. Occasionally I climbed and shook the trees.

They grew also behind my house, and one large tree, which almost overshadowed it, was, when in flower, a bouquet which scented the whole neighbourhood, but the squirrels and the jays got most of the fruit; the last coming in flocks early in the morning and picking the nuts out of the burrs before they fell.

From America to Africa. The word oasis has become so widely understood as an area of perfection in any kind of wilderness that we may well turn to the description by Norman Douglas of the real thing, the gardens of Nefta, with their surprising prodigality.

For the last two days a sand-storm of unusual violence has been raging. On the ridges above the town one can hardly stand on one's feet; the grains fly upwards, over the crest of the hill, in blinding showers, mighty squadrons of them careering across the plain below. The landscape is involved in a dim, roseate twilight. But occasionally there comes a sickly radiance from behind the curtain of a cloud that glimmers lustreless, like an incandescent lamp seen through a fog: it is the sun shining brightly in the pure regions of the upper air.

Here, under the trees, the wind is scarce felt, though you can perceive it by the fretful clashing of the palm branches overhead. And despite the storm, there is a strange hush in the air, the hush of things to come, a sense of uneasiness; spring is upon us, buds are unfolding and waters drawn up forcefully from a soil which seems to heave under one's very feet. It is a moment of throbbing intensity.

And the scirocco moans to these pangs of elemental gestation which man, the creature of earth, still darkly feels within him.

The ground is cultivated with mathematical parsimoniousness and divided into squares which made me think of Roman *agrimensores*. But concerning this point, a civilized old native told me the following legend. Long ago, he said, these oases were wild jungles, and the few human creatures who lived near them little better than beasts. Then came a wise man who cut up and ploughed the watery district of Gafsa, Tozeur and Nefta; he planted trees and all the other growths useful to mankind; he divided the land into patches, led the water through them, and apportioned them among certain families—in short, he gave these oases their present shape, and did his work so well that up to this day no one has been able to suggest any improvements or to quarrel with his arrangement. The story interested me; it may be a variant of the old Hercules myth—it shows how much the Arabs, with their veneration for past heroes and prophets, and their sterile distrust in the possibility of any kind of progress will believe.*

Yet the *deglat* palms which grow here in great abundance—the finest in the world—with their lower leaves pendent, sere and yellow; the figs, lemons, apricots and pomegranates clustering in savage meshes of unpruned boughs, among which the vine, likewise unkempt, writhes and clambers liana-fashion, in crazy convolutions—all these things conspire to give to certain parts of the oasis, notwithstanding its high cultivation, a bearded, primeval look. The

* The author adds a footnote saying that he later learned such a man did, in fact, exist.

palms, particularly the young ones, are assiduously tended and groomed by half-naked gardeners who labour in the moist earth by relays, day and night.

What nights of brooding stillness in summer, under the palms, when those leaves hang motionless in the steaming vapour as though carved out of bronze, while the surrounding desert exhales the fiery emanations of noontide, often 135 degrees in the shade. For the heat of Nefta is hellish.

By way of contrast to this vivid modern description of almost primeval conditions of fruit culture here is a summing up of the pleasures of an orchard in seventeenth-century England by Ralph Austen, author of *A Treatise of Fruit Trees*, 1653:

It is a pleasure to the Eare to heare the sweet notes and tunes of singing Birds, whose company a man shall be sure to have in an Orchard, which is more pleasant there, than elsewhere, because of other concurrent pleasures there; a Consort of Musicke is more pleasant than a single Instrument. . . .

And besides, something more this sense may receive from an Orchard . . . by hearing the slow motion of Boughes and Leaves, by soft and gentle aires, sometimes (as it were) with a kind of singing or whistling noise, which will easily induce a sweet and pleasant sleep in sommer time (if a man be dispos'd) in some close coole Arbor or shady seat.

Secondly the sence of Touch may have more pleasure in an Orchard from the coole fruits, and leaves of Trees, smoothing and brushing the face therewith, which is refreshing and cooling in heat of Sommer. But this sense receives pleasure chiefly by the shade of Trees in Sommer time. Coole refreshing Ayres are found in close Walks, Seats and Arbours under and about the Trees, which keepe off the burning heat of the Sunne. . . .

Thirdly, the sense of Sight partakes of Pleasure in an Orchard, in beholding the exact Order in planting of the Trees, their decent Formes, the well composed Allies, Walks, Seats and Arbours therein; for order and curious formes of things much delight the sight: of this see L. Bacon at large.

Likewise the sight is delighted with pleasant and delicate Colours of the Leaves, Blossomes, and Fruits, that shew themselves in great variety. Curious Colours, especially the Colour greene is accounted helpfull to the sight. . . .

Is it not a pleasant sight to behold a multitude of Trees round about, in decent forme and order, bespangled and gorgeously apparelled with greene Leaves, Bloomes, and goodly Fruits, as with a rich Robe of imbroidered work, or as hanging with some pretious and costly Jewels, or Pearles, the Boughes laden, and burdened, bowing downe to you, and freely offering their ripe fruits, as a large satisfaction of all your labours? . . .

Fourthly, the sense of smell, may likewise have its share of pleasure in a Garden of Fruit-trees. . . . Chiefly the Pleasure this sense meets with is from the sweet smelling blossomes of all the fruit trees, which from the time of their breaking forth, till their fall, breathe out a most pretious and pleasant odour; perfuming the aire throughout all the Orchard. . . .

Fiftly, the sense of Taste has its pleasure in an Orchard. This sense meets with Pleasure at all times of the Yeare from the fruits of an Orchard. . . . The ordinary food they afford all the yeare, and the more delicate for Banquets, are also good and healthfull to the body, as well as pleasant to the tast.

And now to our representative of what are called not fruits but 'vegetables'. The garden pea was found in the ruins of Troy. But it was an undistinguished vegetable until the English squire Thomas Andrew Knight bred the first wrinkled form early in the nineteenth century. It appears in pictures and particularly in wood-carvings of the seventeenth century, where it is said, quite incorrectly, to indicate the work of Grinling Gibbons. But reference to it in poetry is surely unusual. Let us therefore salute Henry Jones, who included in his *Poems on Several Occasions* (1749) the following lines 'On a Fine Crop of Peas being Spoil'd by a Storm'. The poem, as will be seen, exudes a charming Jones-like morality:

> When Morrice views his prostrate Peas,
>   By raging Whirlwinds spread,
> He wrings his Hands, and in amaze
>   He sadly shakes his Head.

FRUITS OF THE EARTH

Is this the Fruit of my fond Toil,
　　My Joy, my Pride, my Chear!
Shall one tempestuous Hour thus spoil
　　The Labours of a Year!

Oh! what avails, that Day by Day
　　I nurs'd the thriving Crop,
And settl'd with my Foot the Clay,
　　And rear'd the social Prop!

Ambition's Pride had spur'd me on
　　All Gard'ners to excel;
I often call'd them one by one,
　　And boastingly would tell,

How I prepar'd the furrow'd Ground,
　　And how the Grain did sow,
Then challeng'd all the Country round
　　For such an early Blow.

How did their Bloom my Wishes raise!
　　What Hopes did they afford,
To earn my honour'd Master's Praise,
　　And crown his chearful Board!

Poor Morrice, wrapt in sad Surprise,
　　Demands in sober Mood,
Should Storms molest a Man so wise,
　　A Man so just and good?

Ah! Morrice, cease thy fruitless Moan,
　　Nor at Misfortunes spurn,
Misfortune's not thy Lot alone;
　　Each Neighbour has his Turn.

Thy prostrate Peas, which low recline
　　Beneath the Frowns of Fate,
May teach much wiser Heads than thine
　　Their own uncertain State.

The sprightly Youth in Beauty's Prime,
    The lovely Nymph so gay,
Oft Victims fall to early Time,
    And in their Bloom decay.

In vain th' indulgent Father's Care,
    In vain wise Precepts form:
They droop, like Peas, in tainted Air,
    Or perish in a Storm.

There are certain other garden delights to be harvested which many gardeners observe only in an almost subconscious manner. To them, writers and artists have paid but little attention. Scent is often referred to as a general attribute of plants and flowers, yet few writers—perhaps they are not skilful enough—have attempted any careful description of a most subtle subject. There are garden sounds. Seldom do most of us consider them, yet, if we pause to think, we realize how many there are and how inseparable from the complete conception of a garden. Even in the closed-in silence of a dense November fog we can still hear a leaf making minute crashes as it falls through the branches. The sense of touch is almost totally ignored, yet surely anyone with the slightest gift of green fingers is acutely, if unexpressively, aware of it.

Few writers can have considered the scents of flowers with greater sensibility than Jason Hill:

There is a way in which we can add another dimension altogether to the garden—and that is by thinking in terms of our sense of smell. The Cinderella of the senses opens the door upon an aspect of reality which most people ignore a little contemptuously, yet the scent of flowers is no small part of their beauty, and by giving a little special attention to it we can have a garden within a garden, an invisible garden not much less rich and various than the other which appeals to the eye.

The right of fragrance to be considered as an independent form of beauty is justified on two grounds: firstly by the tendency of many scents to drift away from the plant that produces them, and, secondly, by the frequent disparity between a plant and its scent. The scent which seems, more than all others, to have an independent existence is that of 'strawberry leaves dying with an excellent cordial smell';

in fact, when I met it for the first time, as I was walking along a country lane in winter, I felt sure that some violets were flowering before their time in the hedgebank, and when I found nothing among the dead leaves to account for the unexpected scent, I was inclined to put it down as an hallucination. There is a distinct note of violet, or rather of orris root in it, together with cedar wood and something like the dry, earthy fragrance of ambergris; and, because all scents of the musk and violet group fatigue our sense of smell very quickly, it seems to fade away almost as soon as you perceive it. This natural elusiveness enabled old Lady Ludlow, in Mrs Gaskell's story, to maintain that it was perceptible only to the members of certain old and aristocratic families, while a later generation, failing to find it in their strawberry beds and reluctant to write themselves off as hopelessly plebeian, seems to have decided that the scent of dying strawberry leaves is a myth. But it is there, for anyone who cares to look for it, in the Wild Strawberry, the Alpine Strawberry and the Hautbois, which were the only varieties known to Elizabethan gardens: and it may even be extracted from their brown leaves, though in confinement it loses a little of its October morning freshness and acquires a hint of Russian leather. The best way to have it in the garden is to let the double form of the Wild Strawberry carpet the ground under some trees, which it will do with great willingness, or to make an edging of one of the improved varieties of the Alpine Strawberry in the kitchen garden.

The secret of dying strawberry leaves is nearly matched by the fragrance which *Veronica cupressoides* gives off in damp weather or when it is wet with dew; but here the note of cedar wood predominates, and the effect is almost exactly that of Vetivert or Khus-Khus, the grass-root which they weave into mats in India. . . .

A variation on the violet theme is played by Mignonette, which introduces a note—a dusty odour of antiquity—that is almost peculiar to itself, though it occurs again, I think, in the subtle chord by the flowers of the Vine and of the Climbing Asparagus, *A. tenuifolia*, which wreathes the groves of Oleander and Lentisc on the shores of the Mediterranean. These plants not only throw their scent far abroad, but seem to disclaim it by the inconspicuousness of their minute greenish flowers.

Edward Thomas expresses the same kind of sensibility in his poem 'Digging':

To-day I think
Only with scents,—scents dead leaves yield,
And bracken, and wild carrot's seed,
And the square mustard field;

Odours that rise
When the spade wounds the root of tree,
Rose, currant, raspberry, or goutweed,
Rhubarb or celery;

The smoke's smell, too,
Flowing from where a bonfire burns
The dead, the waste, the dangerous,
And all to sweetness turns...

The great Gertrude Jekyll had to abandon her work as an artist because of failing eyesight, but found great solace in her very keen hearing:

When I hear a little rustling rush in the grass and heath, or in the dead leaves under the trees, I can tell whether it is snake or lizard, mouse or bird. Many birds I am aware of only by the sound of their flight.

I can nearly always tell what trees I am near by the sound of the wind in their leaves, though in the same tree it differs much from spring to autumn, as the leaves become of harder and drier texture. The birches have a small, quick, high-pitched sound; so like that of falling rain that I am often deceived into thinking it really is rain, when it is only their own leaves hitting each other with a small rain-like patter. The voice of oak leaves is also rather high-pitched, though lower than that of birch. Chestnut leaves in a mild breeze sound much more deliberate; a sort of slow slither. Nearly all trees in gentle wind have a pleasant sound, but I confess to a distinct dislike of the noise of all the poplars; feeling it to be painfully fussy, unrestful, and disturbing. On the other hand, how soothing and delightful is the murmur of Scotch firs both near and far. . . .

The giant grasses, reeds, and bamboo sound curiously dry. The great reed, *Arundo donax*, makes more noise in a moderate breeze than when the wind blows a gale, for then the long ribbon-like leaves are blown straight out and play much less against each other; the Arabs say, 'It whispers in the breeze and is silent in the storm.'

But of all the plants I know, the one whose foliage has the strongest sound is the Virginian allspice (*Calycanthus floridus*), whose leaves are of so dry and harsh a quality that they seem to grate and clash as they come together.

How the other senses can be employed, when one lacks the two most valued, hearing and vision, has been movingly described by the blind and deaf Helen Keller:

Everything that could hum, or buzz, or sing, or bloom, had a part in my education—noisy-throated frogs, katykids and crickets held in my hand until, forgetting their embarrassment, they trilled their reedy note, little downy chickens and wildflowers, the dogwood blossoms, meadow-violets and budding fruit trees. I felt the bursting cotton-bolls and fingered their soft fibre and fuzzy seeds; I felt the low soughing of the wind through the cornstalks, the silky rustling of the long leaves. . . .

Sometimes I rose at dawn and stole into the garden while the heavy dew lay on the grass and flowers. Few know what joy it is to feel the roses pressing softly into the hand, or the beautiful motion of the lilies as they sway in the morning breeze. Sometimes I caught an insect in the flower I was plucking, and I felt the faint noise of a pair of wings rubbed together in a sudden terror, as the little creature became aware of a pressure from without.

Another favourite haunt of mine was the orchard, where the fruit ripened early in July. The large, downy peaches would reach themselves into my hand, and as the joyous breezes flew about the trees the apples tumbled at my feet. Oh, the delight with which I gathered up the fruit in my pinafore, pressed my face against the smooth cheeks of the apples, still warm from the sun, and skipped back to the house!

Yet other delights remain, sometimes noted by the gardener, but often unrecorded by poets and artists. There is an exception in Andrew Marvell, who missed so little in the garden, and wrote finely about the dew:

> See how the Orient Dew,
> Shed from the Bosom of the Morn
> Into the blowing Roses,

DEW

Yet careless of its Mansion new;
For the clear Region where t'was born
    Round in its self incloses!
And, in its little Globes Extent,
Frames as it can its native Element—
    How it the purple flow'r does slight,
Scarce touching where it lyes,
But gazing back upon the Skies,
    Shines with a mournful Light,
       Like its own Tear,
Because so long divided from the Sphear.

Restless it roules and unsecure,
Trembling lest it grow impure,
Till the warm Sun pitty its Pain
And to the Skies exhale it back again.
    So the Soul, that Drop, that Ray
Of the clear Fountain of Eternal Day,
Could it within the humane Flow'r be seen
    Remembring still its former height,
Shuns the sweet leaves and blossoms green;
    And, recollecting its own Light,
Docs, in its pure and circling thoughts, express
The greater Heaven in a Heaven less . . .

5

The Oriental Vision

No writer has described the gardens of Persia with greater gusto than
Sir Robert Ker Porter, who visited the country in the early years of the
last century. The fact that he was an artist of no ordinary kind—his
painting of the Storming of Seringapatam exhibited in 1800 was 120
feet long—and that he married a Russian princess indicate that he had
not that insular view of Persia taken by other travellers who had visited
her gardens. This is his description of the palace of Tackt-i-Kajer:

> It stands on an eminently pleasant point of the adjoining mountains,
> being built on a detached, and commanding hill, on the great slope
> of the Elborz. The edifice is lofty, and when seen from a distance,
> presents a very magnificent appearance. The stateliness of the
> structure itself, is very much increased in effect, by the superb
> ranges of terraces, which connect its spacious gardens, as they
> diverge from the base of the building, downwards, towards the bot-
> tom of the hill. They are laid out in parallel walks, planted with
> luxuriant poplars, willows, and fruit-trees of various kinds, besides
> rose trees in profusion.
>
> In the centre of these shady labyrinths, stands a kind of grotto or
> temple, which, from its construction, materials, and distribution of
> water, must, in summer, be delightful from its coolness and seclu-
> sion. Few of the flowers were in bud, when I first visited this
> charming spot; but the balmy season, advancing with singular rapid-
> ity in these high tracts of Persia, soon covered every mountain's
> brow with rich herbage, and filled the whole air with perfume from
> the full-blown gardens. . . .
>
> One of the most delicious spots to which I paid the most frequent
> visits, after the commencement of the genial weather I speak of,
> was the garden of Negauristan, another palace of the King's. . . .
> The general character of the garden, is like that of Tackt-i-Kajer,

only the grand avenue up the centre of this, is much wider than that of the more distant residence, and is terminated at the higher extremity by a view of the palace; while a Kooleh Frangy, or temple, appears here also between the spacious arcade of trees. Narrow secluded walks, shaded above, and enamelled with flowers below, with cuts of clear and sparkling water, silvering the ground, and cooling the air, vary the scene, from parts which the hand of neglect (or taste, assuming graceful negligence) has left in a state of romantic wilderness. The trees were all full grown, and luxuriant in foliage; while their lofty stems, nearly covered by a rich underwood of roses, lilacs, and other fragrant and aromatic shrubs, formed the finest natural tapestry of leaves and flowers.

On my first entering this bower of fairyland (indeed I may call it the very garden of Beauty and the Beast!) I was struck with the appearance of two rose-trees, full fourteen feet high, laden with thousands of flowers, in every degree of expansion, and of a bloom and delicacy of scent, that imbued the whole atmosphere with the most exquisite perfume. Indeed, I believe that in no country of the world does the rose grow in such perfection as in Persia: in no country is it so cultivated, and prized by the natives. Their gardens and courts are crowded with its plants, their rooms ornamented with vases, filled with its gathered bunches, and every bath strewed with the full-blown flowers, plucked from the ever-replenished stems. Even the humblest individual, who pays a piece of copper money for a few whiffs of a kalion, feels a double enjoyment when he finds it stuck with a bud from his dear native tree! But in this delicious garden of Negauristan, the eye and the smell were not the only senses regaled by the presence of roses. The ear was enchanted by the wild and beautiful notes of multitudes of nightingales, whose warblings seem to increase in melody and softness, with the unfolding of their favourite flowers; verifying the song of their poet, who says: 'When the roses fade, when the charms of the bower are passed away, the fond tale of the nightingale no longer animates the scene.'

At the upper end of the garden, is a small and fantastically built palace, enclosed in a little paradise of sweets. The Shah often retires thither, for days together, at the beginning of summer, before he removes to more distant and temperate regions; and accompanied by the softer sex of his family, forgets, for awhile, that life or the world have other seasons than the gay and lovely spring.

Victoria Sackville-West, herself both writer and gardener, lived in the country just a century after Porter.

All Persian gardens are walled-in. It is part of their character. The Persian, unlike the American, has a feeling for his personal privacy; and, of course, for the privacy of his women: he would never willingly expose his private life to the gaze of the passer-by. So he builds a wall round his garden. Sometimes in the past these walls were elaborated with battlements and with round pigeon-towers at the angles. These pigeon-towers must have added some architectural nobility to the rough blank walls. They are recorded at the four corners of Shah Abbas's Hazar Jarib near Isfahan, and sometimes the wall itself might be decorated with panels of paint or lacquer crowned by a finial in wrought metal. Again, the walls might be used as a support for climbing plants, as in the garden of Karim Khan at Shiraz, where they were clothed on the inside with grape-vines trained on trellises.

Pigeon-towers were not primarily designed for decorative purposes: they were utilitarian in origin. To this day the circular tower, pierced with hundreds of square holes and streaked with whitened droppings, like some sea-girt rock, the refuge of gannets and kitti-wakes, is a frequent object sticking up in the neighbourhood of a Persian village. It recalls the dove-cote or columbarium so often found associated with Tudor manor-houses in England, and has the same charm. But whereas the lady of the manor-house had some affection for her doves or pigeons, coaxing them to peck grain from her hand and to settle without fear on her wrists and shoulders, so that she seemed smothered in a gentle cooing mass of wings and feathers, the Persian takes a far more practical point of view. He eats his pigeons; and above all he collects their dung, a very valuable form of organic manure. The famous melon-garden at Isfahan depended upon it; and has depended upon it right back into centuries. Jean Baptiste Tavernier, writing in 1677, notes more than 3,000 of these pigeon towers round Isfahan. Three thousand towers with at least 1,000 pigeons in each! The whole air must have been vocal with cooing and the brush of wings. . . .

A certain monotony must have attended Persian gardens; or perhaps we should say similarity rather than monotony. It would be churlish to complain of monotony in so grateful a sanctuary. But we may safely say that the lay-out was always more or less the

Figures in a Garden. Persian Tiles. Early seventeenth century. From a garden
pavilion in the Royal Palace of Isfahan. *London, Victoria and Albert Museum.*

Indian Miniature. c. 1820. Guler School. *London, Victoria and Albert Museum.*

same: the long avenues, the straight walks, the summer house or
pavilion at the end of the walk, the narrow canals running like
ribbons over blue tiles, widening out into pools which oddly enough
were seldom circular, but were more likely to be rectangular, square,
octagonal, cross-shaped, or with trilobed or shamrock-like ends.
Sometimes these pools were reproduced inside the pavilion itself:
a mirror of water beneath a domed roof, fantastically reflecting all
the honeycomb elaboration of the ceiling. I remember in particular
one such pool with a kind of central throne on which some nineteenth-century Shah might sit, attired in the minimum of clothing,
while the ladies of his harem, similarly attired or unattired, slithered
down chutes from an upper gallery straight into the embracing arms
of their imperial master.

Thanks to modern methods of swimming bath construction, bathing
in gardens has now become so popular that we have forgotten how, up
to the eighteenth century, the garden was the usual place for the bath,
even in the cool northern countries. In the early nineteenth century,
when prudery and improved plumbing finally put the bath (now hot!)
within doors, Sir Robert Ker Porter related with evident pleasure that
this was still not so in Persia:

> The place of greatest attraction to an oriental taste, certainly was
> the summer-bath. It seemed to comprise everything of seclusion,
> elegance, and that luxurious enjoyment, which has too often been
> the chief occupation of some Asiatic princes; and perhaps will ever
> be the favourite recreation with them all. This bath-saloon, or court
> (for it is difficult to give it an exactly appropriate name), is circular,
> with a vast basin in its centre, of pure white marble, of the same
> shape, and about sixty or seventy feet in diameter. This is filled
> with the clearest water, sparkling in the sun, for its only canopy is
> the vault of heaven; but rose-trees, with other pendant shrubs
> bearing flowers, cluster near it; and, at times, their waving branches
> throw a beautifully quivering shade over the excessive brightness of
> the water. Round the sides of the court, are two ranges, one above
> the other, of little chambers, looking towards the bath, and furnished
> with every refinement of the harem. These are for the accommoda-
> tion of the ladies, who accompany the Shah during his occasional
> sojourns at the Negauristan. They undress or repose in these, before

or after the delight of bathing; for so fond are they of this luxury, they remain in the water for hours; and sometimes, when the heat is very relaxing, come out more dead than alive. But in this delightful recess, the waters flow through the basin by a constant spring; thus renewing the body's vigour, by their bracing coolness; and enchantingly refreshing the air, which the sun's influence, and the thousand flowers breathing around, might otherwise render oppressive with their incense.

The royal master of this *Horti Adonidis* frequently takes his noonday repose in one of the upper chambers which encircle the saloon of the bath; and, if he be inclined, he has only to turn his eyes to the scene below to see the loveliest objects of his tenderness, sporting like naiads amidst the crystal stream, and glowing with all the bloom and brilliancy which belongs to Asiatic youth. In such a bathcourt, it is probable that Bathsheba was seen by the enamoured king of Israel. As he was 'walking at evening-tide on the roof of his palace', he might undesignedly have strolled far enough to overlook the *anderoon* of his women; where the beautiful wife of Uriah, visiting the royal wives, might have joined them, as was often the custom in those countries, in the delights of the bath.

Water and geometrical design are also the essentials of the Indian garden. Most famous is the Taj Mahal, the seventeenth-century garden tomb of Mumtaz Mahal, a consciously planned tribute to India's womanhood. The accounts of the carvers of flowers within the building still exist. As for the surroundings, there is Edward Lear's description recorded in his diary of 16 February, 1874:

Came to the Taj Mahal; descriptions of this wonderfully lovely place are simply silly, as no words can describe it at all. What a garden! What flowers! What gorgeously dressed and be-ringed women; some of them very good-looking too, and all well clothed though apparently poor. Men, mostly in white, some with red shawls, some quite dressed in red, or red-brown; orange, yellow, scarlet, or purple shawls, or white; effects of colour absolutely astonishing, the great centre of the picture being ever the vast glittering ivory-white Taj Mahal, and the accompaniment and contrast of the dark green of cypresses with the rich yellow-green trees of all sorts! And then the effect of the innumerable flights of bright green parrots flitting across like live emeralds; and of the scarlet poinciannas and countless other flowers beaming bright off the dark green! The tinker or tin-pot bird ever at work; pigeons, hoopoes, and I think a new sort of mynah, pale dove colour and gray; also squirrels, and all tame, and endlessly numerous. Poinsettias are in huge crimson masses, and the purple flowered bougainvillea runs up the cypress trees. Aloes also, and some new sort of fern or palm, I don't know which. Below the Taj Mahal is a scene of pilgrim-washing and shrines, altogether Indian and lovely.

What can I do here? Certainly not the architecture, which I naturally shall not attempt, except perhaps in a slight sketch of one or two direct garden views. Henceforth, let the inhabitants of the world be divided into two classes—them as has seen the Taj Mahal; and them as hasn't.

The Islamic influence came into Europe through Spain during the Arabian conquest. The Arabians had kept alive something of the great school of Aristotelian botany after the fall of Greece and Rome. In the time of Alexander the Great, Greek schools were founded in Syria, and the Arabians had translated the Syrian texts into Arabic.

C. M. Villiers-Stuart has described how the traditions from these, adapted to Christian and other ideas, are still found in Spanish gardens:

> The gardening of the Alcázar is no mere accidental survival from past ages, but a unique example of traditional planting handed down by many generations of men.
> The names of the plants also recall old associations. All peaches are still 'Flowers of Damascus', even the brilliant camilla-flowered importation with double carmine blossoms beloved of Kew, but despised by the Alcázar gardeners because its fruit is worthless. A later conquest is recalled by the 'Nut of America', a large tree near the pavilion of Charles V, dominating the other trees in the garden.

Mrs Villiers-Stuart went on to point out how many of the plants grown in Spain even in the twelfth century, as recorded by Abu Zacaria, were importations from the East.

With the new importations came something of their symbolism, for gardening, like every other Eastern art, had its symbolic no less than its practical meaning and arrangement, and these memories clung to the transported flowers. After the Moors had been displaced Moslem attributes and Persian floral fancies became emblems of the Christian virtues, and were included in the heraldry of the saints. Glowing roses typified the fire of missionary zeal, the azure fleur-de-lis suggested the calm of celestial contemplation, which aspires above the sky to the 'Immortal Choir'. The Rosa Mariae, the Rose of Jericho, was believed by the pilgrims to the Holy Sepulchre to have sprung up at each resting-place on the flight into Egypt. It was said to have blossomed for the first Christmas, to have closed at the Crucifixion, and reopened on Easter Day.

The white iris of Moslem grave-yards was sacred to the Madonna and the flower of hope, light and power. Its three-fold petals represented the virtues of faith, wisdom and valour. In Spain the lily was adopted by the Knightly Order of Our Lady of Old Time as their crusading device. Henceforward the Lilies of Our Lady became the special mark of Andalucian design, and the jar or vase with the two-branched lily springing from it was known as the Heraldic Arms of the Virgin. The four pierced iron-work vases filled with lilies crowning the corners of the beautiful Giralda Tower are typically Spanish decoration familiar to those who have visited Seville. Over the doorway of the Archbishop's palace, at the foot of the minaret, these arms of the Virgin occur again. The sacred lotus in its water pot, worshipped from earliest times as the flame of life, found in this guise a way into Christian art and legend; the vase holding the lilies took the place of the lota, or Water-pot of the World, from which the Indian flower sprang. Some Spanish artists went so far as to paint Our Lady sitting on a water-lily, like Buddha wrapped in contemplation floating on the lotus of the Good Law.

The vogue for the much more remote Chinese art and Chinoiserie has been explained in many ways. Mrs Elizabeth Montagu, writing from Tunbridge Wells in 1749, gives one explanation:

People in town had met one another so often at assemblies, etc. they hated each others faces, and we had masquerades of great expense and shew; these tired too, and we wanted to be transported to another country. A Venetian masquerade was thought of; it was called a jubilee; and a boat was surnamed a gondola, and people were transported; a jubilee at Ranelagh, and a gondola on the canal.

Chelsea Chinoiserie figure. c. 1760. *London, British Museum.*

Detail from a Chinese sleeve band, nineteenth century.
London, Victoria and Albert Museum (bequeathed by Gertrude Jekyll).

Oh rare! The conductor of this noble amusement repeats the diversion; all people were tired. Thus has it happened in furniture; sick of Grecian elegance and symmetry, or Gothic grandeur and magnificence, we must all seek the barbarous gaudy goüt of the Chinese; and fat-headed Pagods, and shaking Mandarins, bear the prize from the finest works of antiquity; and Apollo and Venus must give way to a fat idol with a sconce on his head. You will wonder why I should condemn the taste I have complied with, but in trifles I shall always conform to the fashion.

Of the immense vogue of the fashion that philosopher of taste, Lord Kames, observed in 1762 that, 'judging by numbers, the Gothic taste of architecture must be preferred before that of Greece, and the Chinese taste before that of either'.

But we are concerned here with gardens and plants, and it is not irrelevant to quote Sir Joseph Banks, the great President of the Royal Society, scientist and traveller, at but a little later date. 'A man need go no further to study the Chinese than the China paper,' he wrote. 'Some of the plants which are common to China, as bamboo, are better figured there than in the best botanical authors I have seen.'

The Chinese attitude to flowers is indicated perceptively by a traveller and author of our own times, Sir Osbert Sitwell, in his book *Penny Foolish* (1935). It is, he says, 'a very different one from the European':

> The peonies, balancing gaily upon their special terraces, beneath an awning to protect them from the fierce sun of the Chinese summer, attain to a hitherto undreamed-of perfection; especially the tree-peonies. In colour they range through every shade from lotus-pink to so deep a purple that it is known as black. The buds have been cut off here and there, and a great art has inspired the whole of the growing of the tree, while the terraces enable the onlooker to view it from a thousand different angles; for that, indeed, is part of the Chinese theory of gardening. Thus a blossoming tree must always be viewed from above, as well as from beneath and at the side, and for this purpose are constructed those miniature mountains of rock which, at times when the trees are not in flower, seem so meaningless. But who that has seen it can ever forget the flowering of a cherry tree, when viewed from this particular unusual altitude? For it

reveals a vista of winged life at which, before, one could only guess from the deep murmur inhabiting it. From above, as the blossoms lie displayed in the sun, you can watch the going and coming, the endless journeying of the bees and the fluttering of the swallow-tail butterflies.

The cultivation of wistaria, too, has attained in China a degree of excellence unknown here, and the blossom is treated in various and original ways. Sometimes an old vine is hung through a lattice, so that each drooping head is framed in a square; sometimes a stout tree has its serpentine branches supported by painted props of wood which look as though they were fashioned of coral, or, again, it is encouraged to writhe over a shallow pool so that it may be mirrored the better. And in these pleasances are found to perfection the natural stones which, in a Chinese garden, so often take the place of statues. Indeed, for a well-shaped, honeycombed piece of natural limestone rock a Chinese connoisseur is willing to pay the most extravagant price.

China was something of a myth throughout the eighteenth century, when Chinoiserie was the rage. A handful of missionaries, and a few traders all of whose movements were circumscribed, were the only people who penetrated beyond the ports. The first gardener and plant collector to visit the country with some freedom of movement was the Scot, Robert Fortune. He wrote admirable accounts of his travels. His disillusion was at first complete.

On the sixth of July, 1843, after a passage of four months from England, I had the first view of the shore of China; and although I had often heard of the bare and unproductive hills of this celebrated country, I certainly was not prepared to find them so barren as they really are. Viewed from the sea, they had everywhere a scorched appearance, with rocks of granite and red clay showing all over the surface: the trees are few, and stunted in their growth, being perfectly useless for anything but firewood. A kind of fir-tree seems to struggle hard for existence . . . but is merely a stunted bush. . . .

Was this, then, the 'flowery land', the land of camellias, azaleas and roses, of which I had heard so much in England? . . .

This country has long been looked upon as a kind of fairy-land by the nations of the Western world. Its position on the globe is so remote that few—at least in former days—had an opportunity of seeing and judging for themselves; and besides, those few were confined within the most narrow limits at Canton and Macao, the very outskirts of the kingdom, and far removed from the central part or the seat of the government. Even the Embassies of Lord Macartney, although they went as far as the capital, were so fettered and watched by the jealous Chinese that they saw little more than their friends who remained at Canton. Under these circumstances much that was gleaned from the Chinese themselves relating to their country, was of the most exaggerated description, if not entirely fabulous. They from the highest Mandarin down to the meanest beggar are filled with the most conceited notions of their own importance and power; and fancy that no people, however civilized, and no country, however powerful, are for one moment to be compared with them.

By the time Fortune returned with a wonderful collection of Chinese cultivated plants (for he became a trusted friend of many Chinese nurserymen) the vogue for Chinoiserie had died down, so that its former exponents, at least in horticulture and gardening, when they could have the real thing, found it no longer in fashion.

Now that dwarfed trees are again the vogue, it is interesting to read Fortune's first account of them. Writing of the gardens of the mandarins:

> They contain a choice selection of the ornamental trees and shrubs of China, and generally a considerable number of dwarf trees. Many of the latter are really curious, and afford another example of the patience and ingenuity of this people. [He had now learned more of their virtues.] Some of the specimens are only a few inches high, and yet seem hoary with age. Not only are they trained to represent old trees in miniature, but some are made to resemble the fashionable pagodas of the country, and others different kinds of animals, among which the deer seems to be the favourite. Junipers are generally chosen for the latter purpose, as they can be more readily bent into the desired form; the eyes and tongue are added afterwards, and the representation altogether is really good.
>
> One of the Mandarins of Ning-po, anxious, I suppose, to confer some mark of favour upon me, presented me with one of these

animals—plants I should say;—but as it was of no real use to me and as my collections of other things were large, I was obliged to decline the present, which he evidently considered of great value, and no doubt wondered at my want of taste.

For a long time, after Fortune's return, only the coastal lands of Cathay were at all well known. It was not until late in the century that the true wonders of the Chinese landscape, and the home of the Chinese flora, were found to be far away from the great estuaries, high up in the land of the sources of the rivers, in the almost forbidden (to foreigners) provinces of western China. Of the scenery, the American explorer and plant collector J. F. Rock wrote in 1926, describing Lower Tebbu-land:

> I have never in my life seen such magnificent scenery. If the writer of Genesis had seen the Tebbu country he would have made it the birthplace of Adam and Eve, for besides an endless variety of conifers there are even apple trees forty to fifty feet tall, but the apples are not the kind that would have tempted Eve.

The first professional plant collector to break through into Western China was Ernest Henry Wilson, who set out from England on 11 April, 1899, instructed by the nursery firm of Veitch to collect the *Davidia*, or dove tree. The pass to this new country was through the Yang-Tze Gorges. Not long before, Charles Maries had gone thus far, but had turned back on the threshold of the botanists' and plant collectors' paradise. Wilson pressed on from Ichang up the dangerous river and triumphed where Maries had despaired. Was it the country around Ichang that caused him to turn back? Augustine Henry, a doctor and customs official, who guided Wilson to the one *Davidia* he had seen, wrote of Ichang:

> Years ago the whole range was covered with dense forests of pine, which now only exist in places here and there, for the wretched agriculturist, and the miserable being who plants potatoes and opium poppies high up on the range to rid his surroundings of the haunts of black bear, wild boar and other depredationists, have burnt and destroyed the forest. How melancholy the tall trees look denuded of their branches, dead poles instead of living timber. . . .

Over a thousand years earlier a Chinese flower lover who was also a
government official was at the same spot. He was the poet Po Chü-i,
who, having displeased his master, was appointed governor of Chung-
chou, a remote place in Szechuan. He spent a few days at Ichang ex-
ploring the rock-caves. Setting out on the same dangerous passage as
Wilson, he wrote his poem on 'Alarm at First Entering the Yang-Tze
Gorges':

> Above, a mountain ten thousand feet high:
> Below, a river a thousand fathoms deep.
> A strip of sky, walled by cliffs of stone:
> Wide enough for the passage of a single reed.
> At Chü-t'ang, a straight cleft yawns:
> At Yen-yü islands block the stream.
> Long before night the walls are black with dusk:
> Without wind white waves rise.
> The big rocks are like a flat sword:
> The little rocks resemble ivory tusks.
> We are stuck fast and cannot move a step.
> How much the less, three hundred miles?
> Frail and slender, the twisted-bamboo rope:
> Weak, the dangerous hold of the tower's feet.
> A single slip—the whole convoy lost:
> And *my* life hangs on *this* thread!
> I have heard a saying 'He that has an upright heart
> Shall walk scathless through the lands of Man and Mo.'
> How can I believe that since the world began
> In every shipwreck none have drowned but rogues?
> And how can I, born in evil days
> And fresh from failure, ask a kindness of Fate?
> Often I fear that these untalented limbs
> Will be laid at last in an un-named grave!

Today many gardens contain plants collected from the wealth of
Szechuan, and it is pleasant to learn (again in Arthur Waley's masterly
translation) that Po Chü-i gained great pleasure from the flowers and
trees whilst exiled in this isolated province:

> I took money and bought flowering trees
> And planted them out on the bank to the east of the Keep.

I simply bought whatever had most blooms,
Not caring whether peach, apricot, or plum.
A hundred fruits, all mixed up together;
A thousand branches, flowering in due rotation.
Each has its season coming early or late;
But to all alike the fertile soil is kind.
The red flowers hang like a heavy mist;
The white flowers gleam like a fall of snow.
The wandering bees cannot bear to leave them;
The sweet birds also come there to roost.
In front there flows an ever-running stream;
Beneath there is built a little flat terrace.
Sometimes I sweep the flagstones of the terrace;
Sometimes, in the wind, I raise my cup and drink.
The flower-branches screen my head from the sun;
The flower-buds fall down into my lap.
Alone drinking, alone singing my songs,
I do not notice that the moon is level with the steps.
The people of Pa do not care for flowers;
All the spring no one has come to look.
But their Governor-General, alone with his cup of wine,
Sits till evening, and will not move from the place!

Gardening came to Japan from China. But the Japanese developed along their own lines, evolving their own style of design and eventually excelling their masters as florists. Japan was opened to foreigners even later than China and the vogue for Japonaiserie did not reach Europe until the latter part of the nineteenth century—to be put in its place by Gilbert and Sullivan in *The Mikado*. An early visitor to Japan, in 1690–2, was the Dutch naturalist Engelbert Kaempfer. In his *History of Japan*, first translated into English in 1728, he commented on the peculiarily enclosed, domestic conventions of the Japanese garden, which

is commonly square, with a back door, and wall'd in very neatly, like a cistern, or pond, for which reason it is call'd Tsubo, which in the Japanese language signifies a large water-trough or cistern. There are few good houses and inns, but what have their Tsubo. If there be not room enough for a garden, they have at least an old ingrafted plum, cherry, or apricock tree. The older, the more crooked and monstrous the tree is, the greater value they put upon it. Sometimes they let the branches grow into the rooms. In order to make it bear larger flowers, and in greater quantity, they commonly cut it to a few, perhaps two or three branches. It cannot be denied, that the great number of beautiful, incarnate, and double flowers, which they bear in the proper Season, are a surprizingly curious ornament to this back part of the house, but they have this disadvantage, that they bear no fruit. In some small houses, and Inns of less note, where there is not room enough, neither for a garden, nor trees, they have at least an opening or window to let the light fall into the back rooms, before which, for the amusement and diversion of travellers, is put a small tub, full of water, wherein they commonly keep some gold or silver fish, as they call them, being fish with gold or silver-colour'd Tails alive. For a farther ornament of the same place, there is generally a flower-pot or two standing there. Sometimes they plant some dwarf-trees there, which will grow easily upon pumice, or other porous stones, without any ground at all, provided the root be put into the water, from whence it will suck up sufficient nourishment. Ordinary people often plant the same kind of trees before the street-doors, for their diversion, as well as for an ornament to their houses.

A pleasing account of a rather more elaborate Japanese garden, written two hundred years later, was given by the American, Lafcadio Hearn, who lived and taught in the country during the eighteen-nineties:

It is paved with blue pebbles, and its centre is occupied by a pond-let—a miniature lake fringed with rare plants, and containing a tiny island, with tiny mountains and dwarf peach-trees and pines and azaleas, some of which are perhaps more than a century old, though scarcely more than a foot high. Nevertheless, this work, seen as it was intended to be seen, does not appear to the eye in miniature at all. From a certain angle of the guest-room looking out upon it, the appearance is that of a real lake shore with a real island beyond it, a stone's throw away. So cunning the art of the ancient gardener who contrived all this, and who has been sleeping for a hundred years under the cedars of Gesshoji, that the illusion can be detected only from the *zashiki* by the presence of an *ishidōrō*, or stone lamp, upon the island. The size of the *ishidōrō* betrays the false perspective, and I do not think it was placed there when the garden was made.

Here and there at the edge of the pond, and almost level with the water, are placed large flat stones, on which one may either stand or squat, to watch the lacustrine population or to tend the water plants. There are beautiful water-lilies, whose bright green leaf disks float oilily upon the surface . . . and many lotus plants of two kinds, those which bear pink and those which bear pure white flowers. There are iris plants growing along the bank, whose blossoms are prismatic violet, and there are various ornamental grasses and ferns and mosses. But the pond is essentially a lotus pond; the lotus plants make its greatest charm. It is a delight to watch every phase of their marvelous growth, from the first unrolling of the leaf to the fall of the last flower. On rainy days, especially, the lotus plants are worth observing. Their great cup-shaped leaves, swaying high above the pond, catch the rain and hold it a while; but always after the water in the leaf reaches a certain level the stem bends, and empties the leaf with a loud plash, and then straightens out again. Rain-water upon a lotus-leaf is a favorite subject with Japanese metal-workers, and metal-work only can reproduce the effect, for the motion and colour of water moving upon the green oleaginous surface are exactly those of quicksilver.

From the earliest times the Japanese have had a highly developed concern for the beauties of nature. Japanese literature, painting, and ceramic art all bear witness to an intense delight in trees, plants, flowers, and the rock formations which were always an integral element in garden design. 'Viewing-parties' have always been a significant social event—the gathering together of friends to 'view' the flowering of the cherry trees or the changing colours of the maple leaves in autumn. Even before the great landscape tradition of the Japanese woodcut was established by Hokusai and developed by Hiroshige (a development that might in some sense be compared with the transformation of landscape art in England by Constable and Turner) there was a whole school of art concerned with birds and flowers—*Kwachō*. And the figurative artists of the popular *Ukiyo-ye* school delighted to decorate their conversation pieces of Japanese social life with peonies in pots, trailing branches of wistaria, or strings of lanterns and bells, hung amongst the trees, which were a characteristic ornament of the garden scene.

Chobunsai Yeishi (c. 1746-1829). The Paeony Garden, with a Girl carrying a
Koto Box. Woodcut in colours. *London, British Museum.*

Paradise Garden. Detail of a painting in oils by an unknown artist of the Upper
Rhineland School. c. 1410. *Frankfurt-am-Main, Städelsches Kunstinstitut.*

6

Landskip and Design

A visual impression of the mediaeval garden is given in a painting by an anonymous artist of the Upper Rhineland School, dating from about 1410, which is in the Städelsches Kunstinstitut at Frankfurt-am-Main. This is a religious picture, and it depicts the Virgin Mary seated in the Garden of Paradise. At this period it was customary to celebrate the cult of the Blessed Virgin with flowers, and St Gertrude recorded a vision in which she saw the Virgin and Child surrounded by angels in a garden 'full of roses without thorns, lilies white as snow, and fragrant violets'. The artist, when depicting such a scene, placed Mary in a walled garden, a *hortus conclusus* which became an image of Paradise, a garden where all the flowers, their taste and their scents, became symbols of heavenly happiness. For all its symbolism, however, the Frankfurt painting would appear to be a remarkably accurate representation of just such a garden as the artist might see with his earthly eyes, the walled garden or orchard to be found alongside almost every castle of the Middle Ages.

For a verbal description of the form and appearance of the mediaeval garden it is conventional—and, doubtless, reasonably accurate—to quote from *The Romance of the Rose*. In the fourteenth century Geoffrey Chaucer translated it into English. The garden he described, with its nutmegs, plenteous almonds, figs, dates, and 'grains of Paradise' (a plant belonging to the tropical ginger family), obviously originated far south of the British Isles. But we must remember lions were then (apparently) still growling, and unicorns were nuzzling, in French gardens.

> The garden was by mesurying
> Right even and square; in compassing
> It was as long as it was large.
> Of fruit had every tree his charge,

But it were any hidous tree,
Of which ther were two or three.
There were, and that wote I full fell,
Of pome garnettys a full gret dell,
That is a fruyt full well to lyke,
Namely to folk whan they ben sike.
And trees there were of great foisoun
That baren nottes in her sesoun
Such as men notemugges call,
That swote of savour ben with alle;
And almanderes gret plente,
Fyges, and many a date tree,
There wexen, if men hadde nede,
Thorough the garden in length and brede.
There was eke wexying many a spice,
As clowe-gelofre, and lycorice,
Gyngere, and greyn de Paradys ...

In places sawe I welles there
In whiche there no frogges were,
And fayre in shadow was every welle
But I ne can the nombre telle
Of stremys small, that by devyse
Myrthe had done come through condyse;
Of whiche the water in rennying
Gan make a noyse full lykyng.
About the brinkes of these welles
And by the stremes over al elles
Sprange up the grasse, as thicke y-set
And softe as any veluet,
Of whiche men myght his lemman ley
As on a fetherbed to play,
For the erthe was full softe and swete.
Through moisture of the welle wete
Spronge up the sote grene gras
As fayre, as thicke, as myster was.
But moche amended it the place
That there the was of suche a grace
That it of flowers hath plente,
That bothe in somer and wynter be.

There sprange the vyolet al newe,
And fresh pervynke riche of hewe,
And flowers yelowe, white and rede,
Suche plente grewe there never in mede,
Ful gaye was all the grounde, and queynt
And powdred, as men had it peynt
With many a fresshe and sondrie flowre,
That casten up ful good savour.

This chapter will be largely concerned with contrasts—even conflicts—of taste, and it is therefore appropriate to set beside Chaucer's romantic picture a more classical view, as expressed by the Italian Alberti, in his *Ten Books of Architecture* in 1485:

To these Delicacies we must add those of well-disposed Gardens and beautiful Trees, together with Porticoes in the Garden, where you may enjoy either Sun or Shade. To these add some little pleasant Meadow, with fine Springs of Water bursting out in different Places where least expected. Let the Walks be terminated by Trees that enjoy a perpetual Verdure, and particularly on that Side which is best sheltered from Winds, let them be enclosed with Box, which is presently injured and rotted by strong Winds, and especially by the least Spray from the Sea. . . .

Nor let there be wanting Cypress-trees cloathed with Ivy. Let the Ground also be here and there thrown into those Figures that are most commended in the Platforms of Houses, Circles, Semicircles, and the like, then surrounded with Laurels, Cedars, Junipers with their Branches intermixed, and twining one into the other. . . .

The Ancients used to make their Walks into a Kind of Arbours by Means of Vines supported by Columns of Marble of the Corinthian Order, which were ten of their own Diameters in Height. The Trees ought to be planted in Rows exactly even, and answering to one another exactly upon straight Lines: and the Gardens should be enriched with rare Plants, and such are in most Esteem among the Physicians. It was a good agreeable Piece of Flattery among the ancient Gardeners, to trace their Masters Names in Box, or in sweet-smelling Herbs, in Parterres. . . . Nor am I displeased with the placing ridiculous Statues in Gardens, provided they have nothing in them obscene.

The garden of northern Europe in the early sixteenth century, the spirit of the Renaissance now impinging on its mediaeval quality, emerges from the dream-like description of John Skelton in 'The Garland of Laurel':

> The clouds began to clear, the mist rarified;
>   In an herber I saw, brought where I was,
> There birds on the briar sang on every side;
>   With alleys ensanded about in compass,
>   The banks enturfèd with singular solas,
> Enrailéd with rosers, and vines engrapèd;
> It was a new comfort of sorrowis escapèd.
>
> In the midst of a conduit, that curiously was cast,
>   With pipes of gold, engushing out streams;
> Of crystal the clearness these waters far past,
>   Enswimming with roaches, barbellis and breams,
>   Whose scales ensilvered against the sun-beams
> Englistered, that joyous it was to behold.
> Then furthermore about me my sight I revol'd,
>
> Where I saw growing a goodly laurel tree,
>   Enverdurèd with leaves continually green;
> Above in the top a bird of Araby
>   Men call a phoenix, her wings between
>   She beat up a fire with the sparks full keen;
> With branches and boughes of the sweet olive,
> Whose fragrant flower was chief preservative.

Although we have plenty of evidence of the increasing number of gardens and gardeners in England during the second half of the sixteenth century, we have little pictorial evidence of the appearance of the Elizabethan garden. Bacon's description in his famous essay is often quoted, but it must be remembered that this gave his own opinions on what should be, not what was. The Elizabethan garden, except for the much greater variety of plants and fruits cultivated, did not vary greatly from its predecessors. The influence of du Cerceau, who was designing gardens in the grandest manner just across the Channel, does not seem to have arrived. Dr John Hall, botanist and poet, wrote of his garden in 1653 in terms that showed little change from past simplicity:

Scene from a Romance. Arras tapestry. c. 1420. *Paris, Musée des Arts Decoratifs.*

Isaac Oliver. Portrait of a Young Man reputed to be Sir Philip Sidney. c. 1590.
Miniature painting on vellum. *Windsor Castle, Her Majesty the Queen.*

> It hedged was with honeysuckles,
> Or periclimenum;
> Well mixed with small cornus trees,
> Sweet briar and ligustrum.
> The white thorn, and the blackthorn both
> With box and maple fine:
> In which branched the briony,
> The ivy and wild vine.

The knot garden was much in vogue. It was a series of rectangles—or sometimes only one—on which was picked out a pattern often reminiscent of 'strap-work', decorations introduced from Antwerp. The designs were picked out in box, rosemary, privet, or even thorn, but seldom, if ever, in yew, which did not come into general use until Restoration times.

The so-called 'prodigy houses', built on the grandest scale by the courtiers of Elizabeth so that they might entertain her in an appropriate manner, showed more of the French style in gardening, as can be seen from plans or account books still remaining. But how few pictures exist to show them! The subject of one of them, among the finest of Isaac Oliver's miniatures, is unfortunately unknown, though the picture has been long known traditionally as a portrait of Sir Philip Sidney seated in front of Penshurst. All that can be said for certain is that its date is before 1617, when Isaac Oliver died, and that the clothing of the young man is of a later date than 1586, when Sidney was killed. The house is unidentified.

The painting shows clearly the colonnade surrounding the garden, which is typical of sixteenth- and early seventeenth-century practice. Possibly it was constructed of wood, and covered over with vines or even roses. Within, the garden is laid out in a geometrical pattern, rather more elaborate than the Elizabethan knots but not comparable with the ornate patterns already used in France by du Cerceau (who died about 1585). When one looks at the trees in the background one is puzzled; today one would say they were Lombardy poplars, an eighteenth-century introduction. Are they Italian cypresses, which would most improbably reach this height in England? Is this garden perhaps an imaginary one?

There will always be those who argue otherwise, but surely it was the

Renaissance garden in Italy which, within a few centuries, leading to the great formal gardens of Le Nôtre, gave us the greatest gardens that have yet been created. In them architecture and horticulture (for, as Miss Georgina Masson has pointed out, the Italian gardens were not always flowerless) of the highest order were on many an occasion combined. The American novelist, Edith Wharton, writing at the beginning of the present century, established the position of the Italian Renaissance garden so:

> The Italian country house, especially in the centre and south of Italy, was almost always built on a hillside, and one day the architect looked forth from the terrace of his villa, and saw that, in his survey of the garden, the enclosing landscape was naturally included: the two formed a part of the same composition.
>
> The recognition of this fact was the first step in the development of the great garden-art of the Renaissance: the next was the architect's discovery of the means by which nature and art might be fused in his picture. He had now three problems to deal with: his garden must be adapted to the architectural lines of the house it adjoined; it must be adapted to the requirements of the inmates of the house, in the sense of providing shady walks, sunny bowling-greens, parterres and orchards, all conveniently accessible; and lastly it must be adapted to the landscape round it. At no time and in no country has this triple problem been so successfully dealt with as in the treatment of the Italian country house from the beginning of the sixteenth to the end of the eighteenth century; and in the blending of different elements, the subtle transition from the fixed and formal lines of art to the shifting and irregular lines of nature, and lastly in the essential convenience and livableness of the garden, lies the fundamental secret of the old garden-magic.
>
> However much other factors may contribute to the total impression of charm, yet by eliminating them one after another, by *thinking away* the flowers, the sunlight, the rich testing of time, one finds that, underlying all these, there is the deeper harmony of design which is independent of any adventitious effects. This does not imply that a plan of an Italian garden is as beautiful as the garden itself. The more permanent materials of which the latter is made—the stonework, the evergreen foliage, the effects of rushing or motionless water, above all the lines of the natural scenery—all form a part of the artist's design. But these things are as beautiful at one season as another;

and even these are but the accessories of the fundamental plan. The inherent beauty of the garden lies in the grouping of its parts—in the converging lines of its long ilex-walks, the alternation of sunny open spaces with cool woodland shade, the proportion between terrace and bowling-green, or between the height of a wall and the width of a path. None of these details was negligible to the land-scape-architect of the Renaissance: he considered the distribution of shade and sunlight, of straight lines of masonry and rippled lines of foliage, as carefully as he weighed the relation of his whole composition to the scene about it.

During the seventeenth century the Italian formal garden was universally regarded as the ideal—indeed it seemed incomprehensible that any other sort of garden could exist. But as the eighteenth century opened the world of fashion made a volte-face. In 1703 Joseph Addison returned from his Italian journey and wrote: 'I have not yet seen any garden in Italy worth taking notice of.'

This revolutionary view, at first restricted to the English, whose young lords were then beginning to make the grand tour as part of their education, within a few decades became *de rigueur*. The English irregular garden soon won the day. Lord Burlington's villas, pedantically true to the Italian formula, were surrounded by William Kent's landscapes imitating Nature—a Gilbertian situation.

The Englishman's views on Italian formality were put with logic and some subtlety by Tobias Smollett in 1765:

> I shall now hazard my thoughts upon the gardens of this country, which the inhabitants extol with all the hyperboles of admiration and applause. . . . In a fine extensive garden or park, an Englishman expects to see a number of groves and glades intermixed with an agreeable negligence, which seems to be the effect of nature and accident. He looks for shady walks encrusted with gravel; for open lawns covered with verdure as smooth as velvet, but much more lively and agreeable: for ponds, canals, basins, cascades and running streams of water; for clumps of trees, woods and wildernesses, cut into delightful alleys, perfumed with honey-suckle and sweet briar, and resounding with the mingling melody of all the singing birds of heaven. He looks for plats of flowers in different parts to refresh the

sense, and please the fancy; for arbours, grottoes, hermitages, temples, and alcoves, to shelter him from the sun, and afford him means of contemplation and repose; and he expects to find the hedges, groves, and walks, and lawns kept with the utmost order and propriety. He who loves the beauties of simple nature, and the charms of neatness, will seek for them in vain amidst the groves of Italy.

In the garden of the Villa Pinciana, there is a plantation of four hundred pines, which the Italians view with rapture and admiration. There is likewise a long walk of trees extending from the garden gate to the palace; and plenty of shade, with alleys and hedges in different parts of the ground. But the groves are neglected; the walks are laid with nothing but common mould or sand, black and dusty; the hedges are tall and shabby; the trees stunted; the open ground, brown and parched, has scarce any appearance of verdure. The flat regular alleys of evergreens are cut into fantastic figures; the flower-gardens embellished with their cypress and flourished figures in box, while the flowers grow in rows of earthen pots, and the ground appears as dusty as if it was covered with the cinders of a blacksmith's forge.

The water, of which there is great plenty, instead of being collected in large pieces, or conveyed in little rivulets and streams, to refresh the thirsty soil, or managed so as to form agreeable cascades, is squirted from fountains in different parts of the garden, through tubes little bigger than common glyster-pipes. It must be owned, indeed, that the fountains have their merit in the way of sculpture and architecture; and that here is a great number of statues which merit attention. But they serve only to encumber the ground, and destroy that effect of rural simplicity which our gardens are designed to produce. In a word, here we see a variety of walks, and groves, and fountains, a wood of four hundred pines, a paddock with a few meagre deer, a flower-garden, an aviary, a grotto, and a fish-pond and in spite of all these particulars, it is, in my opinion, a very contemptible garden, when compared to that of Stowe in Buckinghamshire, or even to those of Kensington and Richmond.

The Italians understand, because they study, the excellencies of art; but they have no idea of the beauties of nature.

In the nineteenth century the French writer Henri Taine discussed nature and formality with great insight when describing the Villa Borghese, which began in the early seventeenth century as a typical Roman villa and garden but which was surrounded by a 'natural' landscape by the Scottish artist Jacob Moore in 1789. There might be two irreconcilables here, but Taine did not think so:

> The Villa Borghese is a vast park four miles in circumference, with buildings of all kinds scattered over it. At the entrance is an Egyptian portico, in the poorest possible taste—some modern importation. The interior is more harmonious, and quite classical. Here is a little temple, there a peristyle, further on a ruined colonnade, a portico, balustrades, large round vases, and a sort of amphitheatre. The undulating surface rises and falls in beautiful meadows, red with the delicate trembling anemone. Italian pines, purposely separated, display their elegant forms and stately heads in profile against the white sky; fountains murmur at every turn of the avenues, and in small valleys grand old oaks, still naked, send up their valiant, heroic, antique forms. . . .
>
> All that is human is limited, and on this account wearies; lines of buildings are always rigid; a statue or picture is never aught but a spectre of the past; the sole objects that afford unalloyed pleasure are nature's objects, forming and transforming, which live, and the substance of which is, so to say, fluid. You remain here entire afternoons contemplating the ilex, the vague, bluish tint of its verdure, its rich rotundity, as ample as that of the trees of England; there is an aristocracy here as there; only grand hereditary estates can save beautiful useless trees from the axe. By the side of these rise the pines, erect like columns, bearing aloft their noble canopies in the tranquil azure; the eye never wearies in following those round masses, commingling and receding in the distance, in watching the gentle tremor of their leaves and the graceful inclination of so many noble heads, dispersed here and there through the transparent atmosphere. At intervals, a poplar, ruddy with blossoms, sends up its vacillating pyramid. The sun is slowly declining; gleams of ruddy light illumine the grey trunks, and the green slopes are sprinkled with blooming daisies. The sun sinks lower and lower, and the palace windows flash, and the heads of statues are lit up with mysterious flames, while from the distance one catches the faint music of Bellini's airs borne along at intervals by the swelling breeze.

The formal garden of Italy had, of course, been copied and developed to a high pitch of sophistication in France. This is how John Evelyn had reacted to it, on 8 February 1644:

> I this day finish'd with a walke in the greate garden of the Thuil-leries, rarely contriv'd for privacy, shade, or company, by groves, plantations of tall trees, especially that in the middle, being of elmes, the other of mulberys; and that labyrinth of cypresse; not omitting the noble hedges of pomegranates, fountaines, fishponds, and an aviary; but above all the artificial echo, redoubling the words so distinctly, and as it is never without some faire nymph singing to its grateful returns: standing at one of the focus's, which is under a tree, or little cabinet of hedges, the voice seems to descend from the clouds; at another as if it was underground. This being at the botome of the garden, we were let into another, which was being kept with all imaginable accuratenesse in reguard of the orangery, precious shrubes, and rare fruites, seem'd a paradise.

The essence of the French formal garden, of princely as well as aesthetically calculated proportions, is to be found in the work of French painters such as Watteau, Fragonard, or Hubert Robert, for they were essentially settings for fêtes. A brief description by Arthur Young, written towards the end of the eighteenth century, when Englishmen in particular no longer admitted to liking formality, gives something of their quality:

> Chantilly!—magnificence is its reigning character; it is never lost. . . . I had been so accustomed to the imitation in water, of the waving and irregular lines of nature, that I came to Chantilly prepossessed against the idea of a canal; but the view of one here is striking, and had the effect which magnificent scenes impress. It arises from extent, and from the right lines of the water uniting with the regularity of the objects in view.
> It is Lord Kames, I think, who says, that the part of the garden contiguous to the house should partake of the regularity of the building; with much magnificence about a place, this is almost unavoidable. The effect here, however, is lessened by the parterre before the castle, in which the divisions and the diminutive jet-d'eau are not of a size to correspond with the magnificence of the canal. . . .

Arthur Young considered Versailles 'as not in the least striking: I view it without emotion'. Though he condescended towards parts of Chantilly, deep in his heart he was convinced, as were all his British contemporaries, that only the English understood gardening.

The exemplar of the English manner was Lord Cobham's garden at Stowe near Buckingham. In each phase of the movement it was transformed by Vanbrugh, Bridgeman, Kent, and 'Capability' Brown to bring it into vogue: it was, and to some extent still is, a palimpsest. No garden has been more written about—to this day it remains a delightful quarry for research.

The general opinion was put into rhyme by the eighteenth-century poet Nathaniel Cotton:

> It puzzles much the sages' brains,
>   Where Eden stood of yore;
> Some place it in Arabia's plains;
>   Some say it is no more.
>
> But Cobham can these tales confute,
>   As all the curious know;
> For he has prov'd beyond dispute,
>   That Paradise is Stow.

Mrs Elizabeth Montagu, the 'queen of the blue-stockings', agreed with the poet when she went there in 1744:

The first of August we went to Stowe, which is beyond description; it gives the best idea of Paradise that can be: even Milton's images and descriptions fall short of it; and indeed a Paradise it must be to every mind in a state of tolerable innocence. Without the soul's sunshine every object is dark; but a contented mind, in so sweet a situation must feel the most 'sober certainty of waking bliss'. The buildings are indeed, in themselves, disagreeably crowded, but being dedicated to patriots, heroes, law-givers, and poets, and men of ingenuity and invention, they receive a dignity from the persons to whom they are consecrated. Others, that are sacred to imaginary powers, raise a pleasing enthusiasm in the mind.

What different ideas arise in a walk in Kensington gardens, or the Mall, where almost every other face wears impertinence! the greater part of them unknown, and those with whom we are acquainted, only discover to us that they are idle, foolish, vain and proud. At

Stowe you walk amidst heroes and deities, powers and persons, whom we have been taught to honour; who have embellished the world with arts, or instructed it in science; defended their country and improved it.

The temples that pleased me most, for the design to which they were consecrated, were those to Ancient Virtue, to Friendship, to the Worthies, and to Liberty.

Not everyone took the same view. On 13 October 1779, John Wesley wrote in his diary:

The buildings called Temples are most miserable, many of them both without and within. Sir John Vanbrugh's is an ugly, clumsy lump, hardly fit for a gentleman's stable. The temples of Venus and Bacchus, though large, having nothing elegant in the structure, and the paintings in the former, representing a lewd story, are neither well designed nor executed.

From temples we could perhaps move on to other garden buildings— to orangeries, gazebos, belvederes, and the rest. We shall content ourselves, however, with that singular affair which enables the gardener to take on the attributes of a troglodyte. In the eighth century in China Tsu Yung wrote of it as a place for meditation:

Deep in a darksome grove their Grotto lies,
And deep the thoughts that now within me rise.
Fronting the door the South Hill looming near,
The forest mirrored in the river clear,
The bamboo bends beneath last winter's snow,
The court-yard darkens ere the day sinks low.
I seem to pass beyond this world of clay,
And sit and listen to the spring-birds lay.

In the sixteenth century the grottoes of French and Italian and even German gardens—with their specialist constructors like de Caus—had become elaborate and sophisticated. They had become play-like worlds where the pagan gods and goddesses and their attendant spirits dwelt. Ronsard wrote of the mysteries of the grotto at Meudon, built by Charles, Cardinal of Lorraine, in 1552:

Apres l'oraison faite, arrivent à l'entrée
(Nuds de testes et de pieds) de la grotte sacrée;
Car ils avoient tous deux et sabots et chapeaux,
Reverant le sainct lieu, pendus à des rameaux.

   Eux devots arrivez au devant de la porte
Salüerent Pallas qui la Gorgonne porte,
Et le petit Bacchus qui dans ses doigts marbrins
Tient un rameau chargé de grappes de raisins;
Ils se lavent trois fois de l'eau de la fontaine,
Se serrent par trois fois de trois plis de vervene,
Trois fois entournent l'antre, et d'une basse vois
Appellent de Meudon les Nymphes par trois fois,
Les Faunes, les Sylvains et tons les Dieux sauvages
Des prochaines forests, des monts et des bocages;
Puis, prenant hardiesse, ils entrerent dedans
Le sainct horreur de l'antre, et, comme tous ardans
De trop de Deïté, sentirent leur pensée
De nouvelle fureur brusquement insensée.

By the time of Alexander Pope the grotto, while still taken seriously,
had become even more sophisticated, and it was showing signs of
being infected with the latest fashion, Science. Pope wrote 'On his grotto
at Twickenham composed of marbles, spars, gems, ores and minerals':

Thou who shall stop, where Thames' translucent Wave
Shines a broad Mirrour thro' the shadowy Cave;
Where lingering Drops from Mineral Roofs distil,
And pointed Crystals break the sparkling Rill,
Unpolish'd Gemms no Ray on Pride bestow,
And latent Metals innocently glow:
Approach. Great Nature studiously behold!
And eye the Mine without a Wish for Gold.
Approach: but awful! Lo th' Aegerian Grott,
Where, nobly-pensive, St John sate and thought;
Where British Sighs from dying Wyndham stole,
And the bright Flame was shot thro' Marchmont's Soul.
Let such, such only, tread this sacred Floor,
Who dare to love their Country, and be poor.

The sparkling world of mineralogy and the author's noble friends have displaced the nymphs and pagan rites of Meudon. Dr Johnson, however, with that searching common sense which he applied to so many subjects, gave a somewhat more prosaic explanation of Pope's 'folly':

> Being under the necessity of making a subterraneous passage to a garden on the other side of the road, he adorned it with fossile bodies, and dignified it with the title of a grotto; a place of silence and retreat, from which he endeavoured to persuade his friends and himself that cares and passions could be excluded.
>
> A grotto is not often the wish or pleasure of an Englishman, who has more frequent need to solicit than exclude the sun; but Pope's excavation was requisite as an entrance to his garden, and, as some men try to be proud of their defects, he extracted an ornament from an inconvenience, and vanity produced a grotto where necessity enforced a passage.

The element of water in gardens has something—perhaps its fluidity or its impermanence—that has fascinated man from time immemorial. Architects, sculptors, and deeply skilled hydraulic engineers have endeavoured to mould it:

> A Wat'ry Heap by a fresh Torrent fed,
> Hoary with Froth, lifts up its reverend Head,
> Whence various Currents falling, their Recoyl
> Makes them, when cold as Ice, appear to boyl.
>
> Out from his Temples in an artful Crown
> Clear Drops like strings of Pearls, come trickling down,
> Which quickly caught, and thence dispers'd again,
> Seem like a Cloud burst into Showres of Rain.
>
> As once Enceladus, our Architect
> Great Heaps on Heaps of Marble does erect;
> And, like a second Moses, when that's done,
> Commands fresh Springs of Water from the Stone.
>
> When Heav'ns are clear, this Man a second Jove,
> From Earth exhales the Waters up above,
> And thence in Cataracts can make them pour
> When in the Sky there's neither Cloud nor Showre.

So wrote Philip Ayres, a minor poet of the Restoration period.

Particularly did the technology of hydraulics and the art of using it for decoration appeal to the age of the Renaissance. The ever-famous water-works at the Villa d'Este have been described many times, but never better than by Montaigne almost four centuries ago—when no doubt he found them a major distraction from considering the symptoms of his ill-health. 'The gushing of an infinity of jets of water checked and launched by a single spring that can be worked from far off, I had seen elsewhere on my trip, both at Florence and at Augsburg,' he wrote, and then proceeded to enlarge on the singular excellences of Tivoli:

> The music of the organ, which is real music and a natural organ, though always playing the same thing, is effected by means of the water, which falls with great violence into a round arched cave and agitates the air that is in there and from it through the pipes of the organ and supplies it with wind. Another stream of water, driving a wheel with certain teeth on it, causes the organ keyboard to be struck in a certain order; so you hear an imitation of the sound of trumpets. In another place you hear the song of birds, which are little bronze flutes that you see at regals; they give a sound like those little earthenware pots full of water that little children blow into by the spout, this by an artifice like that of the organ; and then by other springs they set in motion an owl, which, appearing at the top of the rock, makes this harmony cease instantly, for the birds are frightened by his presence; and then he leaves the place to them again. This goes on alternately as long as you want.
>
> Elsewhere there issues a noise as of cannon shots; elsewhere a more frequent smaller noise, as of harquebus shots. This is done by a sudden fall of water into channels; and the air, labouring at the same time to get out, engenders this noise. All these inventions, or similar ones, produced by these same natural causes, I have seen elsewhere.
>
> There are ponds or reservoirs, with a stone margin all around and many tall freestone pillars above this parapet, about four paces apart from each other. From the head of these pillars water comes out with a great force, not upward, but toward the pond. The mouths, being thus turned inward and facing one another, cast and scatter the water into this pond with such force that these shafts of water come to meet and clash in the air, and produce a thick and continual

rain falling in to the pond. The sun, falling upon it, engenders, both at the bottom of this pond and in the air and all around this place, a rainbow so natural and vivid that it lacks nothing of the one we see in the sky. This I had not seen elsewhere.

How utterly opposed all this was to the aesthetics of water introduced by the English landscape school of the eighteenth century! Water, they held, might be moving and sparkling only if it were in some stony rill or natural cascade; otherwise it must be placid and calm, appearing as some mighty river from around the corner to wind away again to some concealed infinity.

This attitude to water may well be seen from the critic Thomas Whateley's description of 'Capability' Brown's famous sheet at Blenheim (which we may still see). It was written some six years after the undertaking was completed, which enables us to comprehend this masterpiece with the eyes of Brown's contemporaries.

In the front of Blenheim was a deep broad valley, which abruptly separated the castle from the lawn and the plantations before it; even a direct approach could not be made, without building a monstrous bridge* over this vast hollow: but the forced communication was only a subject of raillery, and the scene continued broken into two parts, absolutely distinct from each other.

This valley has been lately flooded; it is not filled; the bottom only is covered with water; the sides are still very high, but they are no longer the steeps of a chasm; they are the bold shores of a noble river. The same bridge is standing without alteration; but no extravagance remains; the water gives it propriety.

Above it, the river first appears, winding from behind a small thick wood in the valley; and soon taking a determined course, it is then broad enough to admit an island filled with the finest trees; others corresponding to them in growth and disposition, stand in groupes on the banks, intermixed with younger plantations.

Immediately below the bridge, the river spreads into a large expanse; the sides are open lawn; on that furthest from the house formerly stood the palace of Henry the Second, celebrated in many

* Sir John Vanbrugh's 'triumphal causeway'.

an ancient ditty by the name of fair Rosamond's Bower; a little clear spring which rises there is by the country people still called fair Rosamond's Well: the spot is now marked by a single willow. Near it is a fine collateral stream, of a beautiful form, retaining its breadth as far as it is seen, and retiring at last behind a hill from view.

The main river, having received this accession, makes a gentle bend, then continues for a considerable length in one wide direct reach, and, just as it disappears, throws itself down a high cascade, which is the present termination. . . .

The castle is itself a prodigious pile of building, which, with all the faults in its architecture, will never seem less than a truly princely habitation; and the confined spot where it was placed, on the edge of an abyss, is converted into a proud situation, commanding a beautiful prospect of water, and open to an extensive lawn, adequate to the mansion, and an emblem of its domain. In the midst of this lawn stands a column, a stately trophy, recording the exploits of the duke of Marlborough, and the gratitude of Britain. Between this pillar and the castle is the bridge, which now, applied to a subject worthy of it, is established in all the importance due to its greatness. The middle arch is wider than the Rialto, but not too wide for the occasion; and yet this is the narrowest part of the river; but the length of the reaches is every where proportionate to their breadth; each of them is alone a noble piece of water; and the last, the finest of all, loses itself gradually in a wood, which on that side is also the boundary of the lawn, and rises into the horizon.

All is great in the front of Blenheim; but in that vast space no void appears, so important are the parts, so magnificent the objects; the plain is extensive; the valley is broad; the wood is deep; though the intervals between the buildings are large, they are filled with the grandeur which buildings of such dimensions, and so much pomp, diffuse all around them; and the river in its long varied course, approaching to every object, and touching upon every part, spreads its influence over the whole.

This was the scene of which Horace Walpole had written in 1760, four years before landscaping was begun: 'The place is as ugly as the house, and the bridge, like the beggars at the old Duchess's gate, begs for a drop of water, and is refused.'

Such examples as still survive in Britain of the great garden landscapes of the eighteenth century are now so much admired that it is surprising to find how strenuously the movement was resisted by certain tradition-alists at the time. For instance, the Rev Samuel Jackson Pratt, writing in the seventeen-eighties, saw the whole trend as a ridiculous affectation:

> No village dames and maidens now are seen,
> But madams, and the misses of the green!
> Farm-house, and farm too, are in deep disgrace,
> 'Tis now the lodge, the cottage, or the place!
> Or if a farm, *ferme ornée* is the phrase!
> And if a cottage, of these modern days,
> Expect no more to see the straw-built shed,
> But a fantastic villa in its stead!
> Pride, thinly veil'd in mock humility;
> The name of cot, without its poverty!
> By affectation, still with thatching crown'd;
> By affectation, still with ivy bound;
> By affectation, still the mantling vine
> The door-way and the window-frames entwine;
> The hawthorn bow'rs, and benches near the grove
> Give place to temples, and the rich alcove:
> A naked Venus here, a Bacchus there,
> And mimic ruins, kept in good repair;
> The real rustic's sweet and simple bounds,
> Quick-set and garden, chang'd to pleasure-grounds,
> And the fresh sod, that form'd the pathway green,
> The strawberry bed, and currant-bush between
> The honey-suckle hedge and lily tall,
> Yield to the shrubbery and high-rais'd wall;
> Then for exotics of botanic fame,
> Of which the lady scarcely knows the name;
> Yet, as with country friend she goes the round,
> She christens them with words of learned sound.
> The wall, in foreign fruits so rich and fine,
> Forms the dessert, when farmer-gentry dine!
> And then for water! geese and ducks no more
> Have leave to puddle round a modern door;
> Fair on the glassy lake they sail in state,

And seem to know a prouder change of fate;
From thence, on china serv'd, they grace the dish,
And vie in honours with the silver fish.

It took the French some time to assimilate the theory of *le jardin anglais*. The Marquis de Girardin was one of the few to apprehend the English manner, and there were those who considered that in his park at Ermenonville he had, with the assistance of Jean-Marie Morel, *architecte-paysagiste*, and the landscape painter G. F. Meyer, produced a scene superior to some English gardens. Certainly Arthur Young, who visited the place in 1787, was delighted with the arrangement of the water:

It consists of three distinct water scenes; or of two lakes and a river. We were first shown that which is so famous for the small isle of poplars, in which reposes all that was mortal of that extraordinary and inimitable writer [Jean Jacques Rousseau]. This scene is as well imagined, and as well executed as could be wished. The water is between forty and fifty acres; hills rise from it on both sides, and it is sufficiently closed in by tall wood at both ends, to render it sequestered. The remains of departed genius stamp a melancholy idea, from which decoration would depart too much, and accordingly there is little.

We viewed the scene in a still evening. The declining sun threw a lengthened shade on the lake, and silence seemed to repose on its unruffled bosom; as some poet says, I forget who. The worthies to whom the temple of philosophies is dedicated, and whose names are marked on the columns, are NEWTON, *Lucem.*—DESCARTES, *Nil in rebus inane*—VOLTAIRE, *Ridiculum*—ROUSSEAU, *Naturam*—And on another unfinished column, *Quis hoc perficiet?*

The other lake is larger; it nearly fills the bottom of the vale, around which are some rough, rocky, wild and barren sand hills; either broken or spread with heath; in some places wooded, and in others scattered thinly with junipers. The character of the scene is that of wild and undecorated nature, in which the hand of art was meant to be concealed as much as was consistent with ease of access.

Even in this example of 'wild and undecorated nature', you observe, there is a temple. Masonry and statuary have, from classical times on-

wards, been among the chief extraneous delights of a garden. Henri
Taine wrote amusingly of that in Cardinal Albani's Roman Villa:

> . . . our grand seigneur is an antiquary. Besides two galleries and
> a circular portico filled with antique statues, there are pieces of
> sculpture of every description scattered about the gardens: carya-
> tides, torsos, colossal busts, gods, columns topped with busts, urns,
> lions, huge vases, pedestals, and their innumerable remains, often
> broken or mutilated. In order to turn everything to account, a wall
> is frequently encrusted with quantities of shapeless fragments. Some
> of these sculptures, such as caryatides, a mask of Antinous, and
> certain statues of emperors are fine; but the greater part forms a
> singular collection. Many of them belonged, evidently, to small
> municipalities and private dwellings; they are workshop stock,
> already familiar to the ancients, and the same as would subsist with
> us, if after a long period of inhumation our stairway statues and *hotel
> de ville* busts should be discovered; they may be regarded as museum
> documents rather than as works of art.

In the days of Le Nôtre sculpture was much more an integral part
of the garden. D'Argenville, the savant who wrote on this period as a
contemporary in 1709 (the translation is by John James, architect of St
George's, Hanover Square) has this to say:

> Statues and vases contribute very much to the embellishment and
> magnificence of a garden, and extremely advance the natural beauties
> of it. They are made of several forms, and different materials; the
> richest are those of cast-brass, lead gilt, and marble; the ordinary
> sort are of common stone, or stucco. Among figures are distinguish'd
> groups, which consist at least of two figures together in the same
> block; figures insulate, or detached, that is, those you can go quite
> round; and figures that are set in niches, which are finish'd on the
> fore-part only.
> There are likewise, busts, terms, half-length figures; figures half
> as big as the life, and those bigger than the life, called *Colossal*, placed
> either on regular pedestals, or such as are more slender, tapering and
> hollowed, or on flat plinths; not to mention the figures of animals,
> which sometimes adorn cascades; as do brass-relievos and mask-
> heads.

Joseph Francis Nollekens. Conversation Piece. 1740. *Mr and Mrs Paul Mellon.*

Hubert Robert. The Swing. 1777.
New York, Metropolitan Museum of Art.

These figures represent all the several deities, and illustrious persons of antiquity, which should be placed properly in gardens, setting the river gods, as the *Naiades*, *Rivers*, and *Tritons*, in the middle of fountains and basons; and those of the woods, as *Sylvanes*, *Faunes*, and *Dryads* in the groves: sacrifices, bacchanals, and childrens sports, are likewise represented in bass-relieve, upon the vases and pedestals, which may be adorn'd with festoons, foliage, moldings, and other ornaments.

The usual places of figures and vases are along the palisades, in the front, and upon the sides of a parterre; in the niches and sinkings of hornbeam, or of lattice-work made for that purpose. In groves, they are placed in the centre of a star, or *S. Andrew's* Cross; in the spaces between the walks of a goose-foot, in the middle of halls and cabinets, among the trees and arches of a green-gallery, and at the head of a row of trees, or palisades, that stand free and detached. They are also put at the lower end of walks and vistas, to set them off the better; in porticos, and arbors of trellis-work; in basons, cascades, &c.

In general, they do well everywhere; and you can scarce have too many of them in a garden: but, as in the business of sculpture, it should be excellent, as well as in painting and poesy (which are its two sisters) I think it more advisable for a private gentleman to be content without figures, than to take up with such as are but indifferent, which do but create a continual longing after this perfection; the expence of which is fit only for princes, and great ministers.

Whatever the style or form of garden design, it relies for what might be called its permanent vegetable furniture on the forms of trees. Some deep instinct for design has throughout long ages resolved the requirement for this into three distinct forms. First, the steeple or flame-like form, secondly the rounded, cumulus shape, and thirdly the gnarled, irregularly bushy form. Poets and philosophers have written of them from early times—in the cult of the landscape during the eighteenth and nineteenth centuries their aesthetics were much compared and discussed—and painters have displayed them.

Only comparatively lately has the foamy silver birch taken a place in the garden, presumably because of its abundance in the Scandinavian countries, whence the inspiration of much modern architecture springs.

Even so, its aesthetic qualities have long been appreciated; in the mid-seventeenth century there was an Italian painter named the Master of the Silver Birch Trees.

But the history of the spire-like cypress—the *cupressus* of the ancients—goes back far, far beyond that. There is no doubt that the choice of this tree was a purposeful one, presumably on aesthetic grounds. As John Evelyn wrote three hundred years ago, '*Cupressus*, the *Cypress-tree*, is either *Stative*, or *Garden-tree*, the most *pyramidal* and beautiful; or that which is called the *Male* (though somewhat preposterously) which bears the small *Cones*, but is of a more extravagant Shape.'

There are still forests of the 'more extravagant' spreading form which man has left untouched (except for the uses of its timber) and it is the tall 'stative' tree that he has chosen for thousands of years to plant in his gardens and around buildings, first in the Mediterranean regions and later in those areas where the climate is soft enough to sustain it.

The cypress originated in tragic circumstances in the days when the Greek gods were on earth. They have caused it to have a strangely mixed association with rites following death and with the prospects of eternal life, both, it is presumed, from the evergreen foliage and the great age to which it will live.

The story is told by various writers, notably Ovid. He tells us that Apollo favoured a fine stag that came daily to be fed either by the god or by his loved and faithful attendant, young Cyparissus. One day the youth was playfully hurling his spear merely for exercise when, unfortunately, it struck and killed the stag which was bounding from the forest expecting to be fondled. Apollo was unable to console the grief-stricken Cyparissus, who flung himself on the ground in despair:

> Praying, in expiation of his crime,
> Thenceforth to mourn to all succeeding time.
> And now, of blood exhausted he appears
> Drain'd by a torrent of continual tears.
> The fleshy colour in his body fades,
> A greenish tincture all his limbs invades.
> From his fair head, where curling ringlets hung,
> A tapering bush, with spiry branches, sprung

Which, stiffening by degrees, its stem extends,
Till to the starry skies the spire ascends.
Apollo saw, and sadly sighing, cried,
'Be, then, for ever what thy prayer implied.
Bemoan'd by me, in others grief excite,
And still preside at every funeral rite.'

Poetically, this reputation came to England before the tree itself (for the true Italian cypress is a rarity here, being too tender). It is associated with the yew and the willow. Herrick wrote an address 'To the Yew and the Cypresse to grace his Funerall':

Both you two have
Relations to the grave:
    And where
The *Fun'rall-Trump* sounds, you are there.

It is inevitably one of William Browne's

. . . trees whose tears their loss commiserate.
Such are the cypress and the weeping myrrh,
The dropping amber, and the refin'd fir,
The bleeding vine, the wat'ry sycamore.
And willow for the forlorn paramour.

In France, too, the sadness maintains. In *Les Jardins* the Abbé De Lille wrote:

. . . et toi, triste cyprès,
Fidèle ami des morts, protecteur de leurs cendres,
Ta tige, chère au coeur, mélancolique et tendre,
Laisse la joie au myrte, et la gloire au laurier.
Tu n'est point l'arbre heureux de l'amant, du guerrier,
Je le sais; mais ton deuil compatit à nos peines.

In Spain the melancholy attributes of the cypress are offset by the nearby planting of the Judas tree (or, more pleasantly and accurately, the Judaean tree). This, with its pink flowers borne precariously on the bare trunks and shoots, symbolizes the more fleeting joys in life. It is the *arbor del amor*.

The literary allusions to the cypress are still so widely comprehended that D. H. Lawrence had only to write:

> Along the avenue of cypresses,
> All in their scarlet cloaks and surplices
> Of linen, go the chanting choristers,
> The priests in gold and black, the villagers.

and a whole scene was set.

Yet in spite of these traditions of gloom, the cypress remains the most significant tree in Western garden design. Where it will not thrive, we have hardier North American trees of rather similar form, such as Lawson's cypress and the incense cedar, to replace it.

Always it has attracted and affected painters. The Italian primitives have it standing stiffly in the landscapes and around their tidy gardens; it is often in the paintings of the later Italian masters, abounds in the pictures of Claude and Poussin, is frequent in the landscapes of Turner, Wilson, and the English water-colourists who went to Italy, and was studied intensely by Van Gogh:

> The cypresses are always haunting me; I would like to make something of them like the canvases of sunflowers, because it astonishes me they have not yet been done the way I see them. In line and in proportion as beautiful as an Egyptian obelisk. And the green has such a quality apart. It is a spot of *black* in a sunlit landscape, but of a shade of black the most interesting and the most difficult to his exactly, that I can imagine. But then you must see them here against the blue—in the blue rather.

At St Rémy he painted at least ten canvases dominated by cypresses. His preoccupation with the subtle colours of conifers which can, from a distance, turn black, is unusual. This phenomenon is well displayed far north from the Mediterranean. Within Scotland's famed Black Wood of Rannoch so various are the colours that one is perplexed by the name. Yet how well is it justified when one sees it, even on the sunniest days, from the far side of the loch.

The stone-pine has not attained such prominence in literature, though

Vincent van Gogh. Ladies in a Garden Landscape. 1890. *Amsterdam, Stedelijk Museum.*

Jean Honoré Fragonard. Blind Man's Buff (in the garden of the Villa d'Este). Detail.
Washington, National Gallery of Art : Samuel H. Kress Collection.

it has from ancient times provided the rounded contrast to the cypress. It was Wordsworth's tree on Monte Mario at Rome—

> I saw far off the dark top of a pine
> Look like a cloud—a slender stem, the tie
> That bound it to the native earth . . .

Like the cypress, man has planted it so extensively that its original territory is now unknown. Unlike the cypress, these travels had utilitarian motives. The timber was used in classical times for ship-building, and the cone—the original pineapple—we have discussed elsewhere.

Aesthetically, the 'sailing pine' really came into its own with the paintings of Claude, who so often used it in those scenes that inspired Richard Wilson and other artists of the English landscape school. The stone-pine was, somewhat incongruously (for a tree so closely associated with the classical formal garden), associated by the eighteenth-century Joseph Warton with 'Nature'—

> Rich in her weeping Country's Spoils *Versailles*
> May boast a thousand Fountains, that can cast
> The tortur'd Waters to the distant Heav'ns;
> Yet let me choose some Pine-topt Precipice
> Abrupt and shaggy, whence a foamy Stream,
> Like Anio, tumbling roars; or some bleak Heath,
> Where straggling stand the mournful Juniper,
> Or Yew-tree scath'd . . .

This accords with the spirit that admired the irregularity of the oak; and particularly the Spanish chestnut. As the Rev William Gilpin wrote in the 1790s, the chestnut is,

> in maturity and perfection, a noble tree; that grows not unlike the oak. Its ramification is more straggling; but it is easy, and its foliage loose. This is the tree which graces the landscapes of Salvator Rosa. In the mountains of Calabria, where Salvator painted, the chestnut flourished. There he studied it in a thousand beautiful shapes, as the exigences of his composition required. I have heard indeed that

it is naturally brittle, and liable to be shattered by winds; which might be one reason for Salvator's attachment to it.

There are other garden trees of singular form and character that do not belong to the classical age. Such is the horsechestnut—a newcomer. It did not arrive, by a devious route, from the Balkans until the seventeenth century. Gilpin considered it 'a heavy, disagreeable tree. . . . This tree is however chiefly admired for its flower, which *in itself* is beautiful: but the whole tree together in flower is a glaring object, totally unharmonious, and unpicturesque.'

That was not the opinion of the fastidious Le Nôtre, who planted it widely in his avenues. Nor is it the opinion of the common man, who delights in its glories, and still less of his son who later gathers the 'conkers'. And for others, too, such as the poet William Kerr, it is a symbol of the eternally recurring joy of a season tinged with melancholy as age begins to possess us:

> Chestnut candles are lit again
> For the dead that died in spring:
> Dead lovers walk the orchard ways,
> And the dead cuckoos sing.
>
> Is it they who live and we who are dead?
> Hardly the springtime knows
> For which today the cuckoo calls,
> And the white blossom blows.
>
> Listen and hear the happy wind
> Whisper and lightly pass:
> 'Your love is sweet as hawthorn is,
> Your hope green as the grass.
>
> 'The hawthorn's faint and quickly gone,
> The grass in autumn dies:
> Put by your life, and see the spring
> With everlasting eyes.'

Before we turn from the trees, we should pay tribute to the men who, in the nineteenth century, altered the appearance of, not only the garden, but often the woodland scene in much of the temperate and even the sub-tropical world. These were the men who explored and collected on the coasts and up the rivers of Pacific North America. When the foremost of them, the Scot David Douglas, was there in the eighteen-twenties the country and its stupendous trees and forests were known but to a handful of men other than the Indians. During his hard-pressed and dangerous life he again and again paused breathlessly to describe the vast landscape in his *Journal*. Near the Grand Rapids he wrote:

> The scenery . . . is grand beyond description; the high mountains in the neighbourhood, which are for the most part covered with pines of several species, some of which grow to an enormous size, are all loaded with snow; the rainbow from the vapour of the agitated waters, which rushes with furious rapidity over sheltered rocks and deep caverns, producing an agreeable though at the same time a somewhat melancholy echo through the thick wooded valley; the reflections from the snow on the mountains, together with the vivid green of the gigantic pines, form a contrast of rural grandeur that can scarcely be surpassed.

The greatest conifer of them all, the giant sequoia, Californian bigtree, was not discovered until later, in 1841. How it first came before the British people and got its English name wellingtonia (every good-sized British mansion still has at least one) raised the prose of the distinguished botanist John Lindley to normally unprofessional heights. One suspects that the Editor of *The Gardener's Chronicle* held the article till his issue of Christmas Eve 1853, so that gardeners would have a great deal to talk about during the holiday.

Professor Lindley opened in a disarmingly off-hand manner.

> The other day, we received from Mr Veitch branches and cones of a most remarkable coniferous tree, seeds and a living specimen of which had just been brought him by his excellent collector Mr Lobb, who, we are happy to say, has returned loaded with fine things.

Then follows a rather dull description of these specimens to presage the excitement:

What a tree this is! The specimen felled at the junction of the Stanislau and San Antonio was above 3,000 years old; that is to say, it must have been a little plant when Samson was slaying the Philistines, or Paris running away with Helen, or Aeneas carrying off good *pater Anchises* upon his filial shoulders. . . . No one will differ from us in feeling that the most appropriate name to be proposed for the most gigantic tree which has been revealed to us by modern discovery is that of the greatest of modern heroes. Wellington stands as high above his contemporaries as the Californian tree above all the surrounding forest. Let it then be given the name *Wellingtonia Gigantea.*

As we move on to features of the natural landscape garden no one concerned with an attempt to design a garden in this style as a work of art (no mean feat) should fail to consider the views of the poet Shenstone, who devoted much of his life to perfecting a single garden, at the Leasowes in the Worcestershire hills. Shenstone was opposed to all that Le Nôtre stood for. Here are some of his *Unconnected Thoughts on Gardening*:

> Perhaps the division of the pleasures of imagination, according as they are struck by the great, the various, and the beautiful, may be accurate enough for my present purpose. . . . There seems however to be some objects which afford a pleasure not reducible to either of the foregoing heads. A ruin, for instance, may be neither new to us, nor majestick, nor beautiful, yet afford that pleasing melancholy which proceeds from a reflexion on decayed magnificence. For this reason an able gardiner should avail himself of objects, perhaps, not very striking; if they serve to connect ideas, that convey reflexions of the pleasing kind. . . .

> It is no objection to the pleasure of novelty, that it makes an ugly object more disagreeable. It is enough that it produces a superiority betwixt things in other respects equal. It seems on some occasions to go even further. Are there not broken rocks and rugged grounds, to which we can hardly attribute either beauty or grandeur, and yet when introduced near an extent of lawn, impart a pleasure equal to more shapely scenes? Thus a series of lawn, though ever so beautiful, may satiate and cloy, unless the eye passes to them from wilder scenes; and then they acquire the grace of novelty. . . .

Ground should first be considered with an eye to its peculiar character: whether it be the grand, the savage, the sprightly, the melancholy, the horrid or the beautifull. As one or other of these characters prevail, one may somewhat strengthen its effect, by allowing every part some denomination, and then supporting it's title by suitable appendages—For instance, The lover's walk may have assignation seats with proper mottoes—Urns to faithful lovers—Trophies, garlands, &c. by means of art. . . .

I use the words landskip and prospect, the former as expressive of home scenes, the latter of distant images. Prospects should take in the blue distant hills; but never so remotely, that they be not distinguishable from clouds. Yet this mere extent is what the vulgar value. . . .

Landskip should contain variety enough to form a picture on canvas; and this is no bad test, as I think the landskip painter is the gardiner's best designer. The eye requires a sort of ballance here; but not so as to encroach upon probable nature. A wood, or hill, may ballance a house or obelisk; for exactness would be displeasing. We form our notions from what we have seen; and though, could we comprehend the universe, we might perhaps find it uniformly regular; yet the portions that we see of it, habituate our fancy to the contrary. . . .

It is always to be remembered in gardening that sublimity or magnificence, and beauty or variety, are very different things. Every scene we see in nature is either tame and insipid; or compounded of those. It often happens that the same ground may receive from art, either certain degrees of sublimity and magnificence, or certain degrees of variety and beauty; or a mixture of each kind. In this case it remains to be considered in which light they can be rendered most remarkable, whether as objects of beauty, or magnificence. Even the temper of the proprietor should not perhaps be wholly disregarded; for certain complexions of soul will prefer an orange tree or a myrtle to an oak or cedar. However, this should not induce a gardiner to parcel out a lawn into knots of shrubbery; or invest a mountain with a garb of roses. This would be like dressing a giant in a sarsenet gown, or a saracen's head in a brussels nightcap. . . .

Dr Johnson, however, summed up the Shenstonian philosophy thus:

He began from this time to point his prospects, to diversify his surface, to entangle his walks, and to wind his waters, which he did with such judgement and fancy as made his little domain the envy of the great and the admiration of the skilful—a place to be visited by travellers and copied by designers. Whether to plant a walk in undulating curves, and to place a bench at every turn where there is an object to catch the view, to make water run where it will be heard, and to stagnate where it will be seen; to leave intervals where the eye will be pleased, and to thicken the plantation where there is something to be hidden—demands any great powers of mind, I will not enquire; perhaps a surly and sullen speculator may think such performances rather the sport than the business of human reason.

In spite of Dr Johnson, Shenstone's ideas prevailed until the return of formality and bedding-out in the nineteenth century. But before we consider the problems of the Victorian garden we should listen to a few fine phrases and noble conceptions uttered by an eminent but by no means representative Victorian gardener, the ingenious and eccentric father of the poetic Sitwells. Here are a few lines from Sir George Sitwell's splendid essay *On the Making of Gardens*:

To make a great garden, one must have a great idea or a great opportunity; a cypress causeway leading to a giant's castle, or a fountain cave where a ceaseless iris plays on a river falling through the roof, or a deep clear pool with an under-world fantasy of dragon-guarded treasure caves lit by unearthly light, or a mighty palace quadrangle lined with hanging gardens of arcaded terraces, or a great galleon in a lake whose decks are dropping with jasmine and myrtle, or a precipitous ravine with double bridges and a terrace on either hand. But it is possible to introduce a touch of imaginative beauty into almost any garden by finding the most perfect form for one of its features, or by giving expression to the soul of some particular flower or tree, as with the Virginian vine on the trellis arcades at Schwetzingen and the cypress in the Giusti avenue at Verona.

So, if it is to be a rose-garden, do not choose those stunted, unnatural earth-loving strains, which have nothing of vigour and wildness in them, nor banish other flowers which may do homage to the beauty of a rose as courtiers to a queen. Let climbing roses drop in a veil from the terrace and smother with flower-spangled embroidery the garden walls, run riot over vaulted arcades, clamber up lofty obelisks of leaf-tangled trellis, twine themselves round the pillars of a rose-roofed temple, where little avalanches of sweetness shall rustle down at a touch and the dusty gold of the sunshine shall mingle with the summer snow of the flying petals. Let them leap in a great bow or fall in a creamy cataract to a foaming pool of flowers. In the midst of the garden set a statue of Venus with a great bloom trained to her hand, or of Flora, her cornucopia overflowing with white rosettes, or a tiny basin where leaden *amorini* seated upon the margin are fishing with trailing buds.

By the mid-nineteenth century the old landscape gardens remained in England, but grafted on to them as often as not were new bits of geometrical formality bedded out with sub-tropical plants. The result was a charming (or sometimes horrifying) confusion. Of the former, there is Percy Lubbock's account of the garden of his old home in Norfolk:

> . . . to right and left, there was a fantastic medley of flower-beds, cut in queer shapes, coils and lozenges and loops; and the gardener's fancy ran strangely riot, year by year, in selecting and disposing the flowers that filled them. Geraniums roasting-red, French marigolds orange and mahogany-coloured, the tomato-note of waxen begonias, exotic herbage all speckled and pied and ring-straked, dahlias, calceolarias—they were marshalled and massed together, they fought it out as they would. But indeed they were mastered by the sunshine, by the blaze of light in which they flashed and twinkled; and they fell back, right and left, leaving a wide space of clear green grass unbroken. And then there rose before you the green bank, so steep that I wonder how the mowing-machine contrived to sidle along it and keep it thus smoothly shaven.
>
> To me, as I gained the crest of the bank, it seemed as though the huge flat of the lawn stretched away and ahead for a mile; so serene, so steady and peaceful it was, with nothing to break its even greenness till the eye, sweeping far, reached the shrubberies and trees that bordered it about. The broad silence made nothing of such trivialities as a lawn-tennis net, a few croquet hoops; they were lost in the quiet plain. Beyond it the horizon was bounded by clumped oaks, by dim woods more distant; out there was the park, and you could catch sight of the cows swinging their tails in the deep pasture. . . .

... under the tasselled branch of a larch that leans out from the edge of the shrubbery, I take in afresh the delightful sense of easy abundance, the loose comfort, the soft-bosomed maturity of the garden. Those lobelia-stripes, those marigold-patches might look harsh and hard, you would think; one knows how smartly odious they can appear in a well-kept garden, so called, where the flowers seem to have been—what shall I say?—to have been stuffed and mounted, lest they should take their ease as living creatures. Not a flower could look constrained, unnaturally smartened, in the garden at Earlham; even if they sat up in rows and stripes, they did so with enjoyment unconcerned. They glowed, they revelled; and moreover it was not, in any vulgar sense, a well-kept garden. It was profusely inconsistent; if one flower-bed was stuck over with geraniums like a pin-cushion and rimmed with horrible little monsters of fretted, empurpled foliage, the next might be a bower, a boscage, a ramp of sweet peas, a bushy luxuriance of phlox and rosemary. And especially the border against the slow curve of the wall which I mentioned just now—this was a mazy confusion of everything that gleams and glows and exhales a spicery of humming fragrance. Peacock butterflies, brilliant red admirals, fluttered over the blue mist of sea-lavender; a tree of verbena, the lemon-scented herb of which you pull a leaf whenever you pass, branched out close to the immense old trunk of the wistaria; salvia blue and red, bitter-sweet phloxes white and crimson-eyed, the russet and purple trumpets of the lovely creature afflicted with the name of salpiglossis, they all rejoiced together, rambling and crowding in liberal exuberance. The gardener might wreak his worst will, scheming for a smart patchwork; but the free soul of the garden escaped him and bloomed tumultuously.

But by now William Robinson had arisen to smite all unnaturalness and bedding out. Miss Jekyll had with more subtlety evolved an entirely new manner of planting in which subtlety of colour and form were combined. Beatrix Farrand was to become an exponent of this manner in North America.

It is not usually remembered that Miss Jekyll was contemporary with the French Impressionist movement and it is not difficult to see many points she had in common with their ideas of the use of colour and sunlight. Claude Monet painted many pictures of his and, indeed, other

James Joseph Jacques Tissot. The Gardener. 1879.

Claude Monet. Monet's Garden at Vétheuil. 1880. *Mrs Mellon Bruce*.

gardens. He was but three years older than Miss Jekyll, and an active gardener. It is said that in 1872 when he and Renoir were hard up they shared a plot of land on which they cultivated potatoes. In the 1870s we have the pictures of his garden at Argenteuil. They are of trees, great free-growing bushes of roses and dappled sunlight on the grass; in the distance his home, which might be an old farmhouse in almost any country. The whole effect is strikingly different from the typical trim, mid-nineteenth-century suburban gardens and remarkably evocative of a corner in a Robinson or Jekyll garden. His patron, Caillebotte, was a passionate gardener, and probably supplied him with plants in his poverty-stricken Argenteuil days.

Later, he moved to Giverny, and again he was helped by the skilful Caillebotte. Here again he had a small farmhouse. In the old orchard he established flowers among the fruit trees. The effect in the lush grass was carefully planned to form an iridescent mixture of colours (he liked, in a *pointilliste* manner, to build up his colour from plants with countless small flowers). Particularly did he form arches of climbing roses—again a feature of Miss Jekyll's garden. By degrees Monet's pictures became well liked, and in the late part of the century those of his garden must have influenced taste. Eventually, as is well known, he bought some waste, marshy land close to his house and near the river. Here he made his water garden, with pools planted with water-lilies mirroring the sky and adjoining trees, and trellised fences of climbing roses. And, of course, his Japanese bridge from which trailed wistaria. In 1900 came his series of twelve big pictures, *Le Bassin aux Nymphéas*, in 1913 his *Arceaux Fleurs*, and in 1918 his *Saule Pleureur*. All these must have had a profound influence on garden design.

Another style of gardening that came in with the end of the nineteenth century we are inclined to forget; it is the type of garden that Edmund de Goncourt described in 1881, standing near the ancient Montmorency Park, some of whose aged trees adjoined it.

> Italy, with her villas, had given me a taste for the 'furnished' gardens, those gardens where objects of bronze, marble, terracotta, and porcelain on every side peer through the green of the

foliage. Instead of antiques . . . I erected at the garden gate a trellis after the model of the eighteenth century, two porcelain terminal statues ending in women's necks, and little smiling cherubs' heads crowned by baskets. At the slope of a staircase, with balustrades and the lower steps carpeted with ivy, I placed two bronze cupids, hailing from a sale of Monbro, of defective workmanship, but of pleasing conceit. At the top of the small lawn I placed a great Japanese crane, with the leg thrown forward and the head back, so life-like upon its water-lily leaf, that once a dog crouched, pointing at its bronze stilts. Into a stone cippus, garlanded with creepers, I had fitted a terra-cotta—it crumbled away, alas, in the air—a low relief of cupids by Angelo Rossi, the powerful and robust sculptor of the Angels at St Peter's at Rome. . . .

Finally, I surrounded my clumps with a frame-work of biscuit porcelain, the invention of which I credit to myself, and shaped some open-worked hoops, which, half buried in the earth, and half crossing one another, form a completely ornamental network. For my favourite nook, my little rock under the great trees, I sacrificed a bit of white Saxe porcelain, a dolphin with the body, snout, and fins modelled amid the ruggedness of a graceful rockery, forming in the centre of the dark vegetation of the fountain a most successful white blotch.

Many treatises have been written on the art—as opposed to the mechanics—of garden design. They may be found devoted to formal, landscape, and latterly the kind known optimistically as labour-saving gardens. Relatively little, however, has been written about the aesthetics of rock, or as they are now rather whimsically called, alpine gardens. There is the general directive that they should be natural, but the art that should find its way into their design has been but little discussed. Robert Gathorne-Hardy has looked at this matter:

The problem to face if you are making a rock garden is whether to have an ostentation of flowers, sweeps of colour with brave harmonies, a sort of park or sea-side garden effect, or else a jeweller's window full of fine, small, exquisite things. Mine is an unfortunate compromise. I had intended to keep the screes and occasional corners for the small divinities, letting bolder things luxuriate over the rest: a pretty plan which nature forbade, sowing, as I have told, harebells and mountain pansies in the screes, or flopping leaf and shoot in gross and unsuspected ardour on to my jewelled ledges. The saxifrages which come under the division *Kabschia* suffer particularly. More audacious beauties shade and smother those tight cushions on which large flowers have glowed in early spring; the neat shoots become pale and lanky, and then, for the most part, rot in the fogs and frosts of winter.

Among the worst of these sinning beauties is *Campanula carpatica*, with its lovely, large, upturned cups in varying shades of blue. And yet, how much *should* I regret it? The rock garden really does make a fine blaze in June. The different rock-roses are in their full glory of red and yellow and white; the silver saxifrages are out, great loose sprays from *Cotyledon*, at least one magnificent fox-tail fountain from *longifolia*, and all the variety of *Aizoon*; the pinks make a fragrant glow, and their cousins *Lychnis* and *Arenaria* and *Silene* and *Gypsophila* in several species, are blooming; and to back it all, the campanulas give every shade and change of the heaven's colours.

At this time, too, a 'weed' is flowering which I never regret. Once when I was staying in France I collected some plants of a campanula having large open stars on delicate sprays. This was *Campanula patula*, a rare native of England. It flowers and seeds itself everywhere, so that any bare patch of rock garden becomes, in high summer, an unbroken glimmering drift of blue. *Campanula patula* is a biennial which never chokes its neighbours, and if it should happen to fall on a vulnerable spot it is easily pulled up. And from its flowers, in the hey-day of them, a new problem of design arises, namely, what spaces to clear, what shadows in a heaven of dusty blue to cut away, so that the general pattern and colour of things shall best be displayed.

Yes, the summer is definitely rather ostentatious, with a gay and lovable vulgarity, like the piers and beaches at Margate or Southsea or Blackpool.

But chaste and gem-like are the flowers which, from the first foretaste of spring, burn and glimmer in this garden. In the cold air of some January morning, when the sun shines as though through a tawny crystal, the springs of colour begin to weep a few jewels from their stirring orifices. Just a few flowers may be seen then of the Asturian daffodil, which sometimes appears even in December; here and there the blue of a *Chionodoxa*, or the white of a blanched scilla;

and the hoop-petticoats will open soon, first the yellow, and then the sulphur-coloured.

This golden early spring on the made slopes may thus begin in January, or even December, and when March goes out it is almost over. At its noon Asturian daffodils blossom in hundreds, while the more delicate-coloured, heavenly fragrant little jonquils from San Juan make paler groups. The white daffodils bloom in one or two clumps, closer together than their wilder brethren on the romantic mountain, their drooping flowers, with a corona of twisted segments, opening cream-coloured and fading to a glassy white; and year by year the angel's tears increase in strength and number, hanging out, as they become established, three, or even four, magical creamy Columbines on curving stems. Meanwhile, the Bayonne daffodils, *Narcissus pallidiflorus*, from Saint-Jean-de-Luz and Covadonga, make a splash of straw-yellow, contrasting with the chocolate bells, sometimes yellow streaked, of *Fritillaria pyrenaica*. And, as on the Spanish mountains, dog's tooths are opening besides the little daffodils. Earth shows at this season like black velvet for jewels to rest on.

This chapter has been concerned with different and often conflicting conceptions of garden design. As every gardener knows, however, plans and plants all too often fail to achieve what is expected of them. To put matters in true perspective, therefore, we end with some cautionary lines addressed to a horticultural friend by an eighteenth-century poet, John Scott:

> Proceed, my Friend, pursue thy healthful toil,
> Dispose thy ground, and meliorate thy soil;
> Range thy young plants in walks, or clumps, or bow'rs,
> Diffuse o'er sunny banks thy fragrant flow'rs;
> And, while the new creation round thee springs,
> Enjoy uncheck'd the guiltless bliss it brings:
> But hope no more. Though Fancy forward stray
> These scenes of distant pleasure to survey,
> T' expatiate fondly o'er the future grove,
> The happy haunt of Friendship and of Love;
> Know, each fair image form'd within thy mind,
> Far wide of truth thy sickening sight shall find.

Ivon Hitchens. Corner of a Garden. 1955. *Miss Sheila McCririck*.

The Garden of Love. Miniature painting on vellum. School of Fontainebleau.
Second half of the sixteenth century. *London, Wallace Collection.*

7
The Garden of Love

Love in all its forms, sacred and profane, has been associated with gardens, fruit, and flowers since that first happening in the Garden of Eden. One of the earliest examples of the influence of profane love in a garden is to be found in the Apocrypha, in the History of Susanna, who was in the habit of walking in her husband's walled garden, and bathing herself after the garden doors had been closed. The lust-inflamed elders, when they subsequently gave false witness against her, convicted themselves of lying by the fact that one of them said she had been 'companying' with her alleged lover 'under a mastick tree' whereas the other declared she was 'under a holm tree'. Daniel, coming to judgement, clearly recognized their botanical inconsistency.

The pure poetry of love is nowhere more eloquently expressed in the Bible than in Solomon's Song. Here the garden allusions are abundant, since Solomon unmistakably visualizes the object of his love as a garden:

> A garden enclosed is my sister, my spouse; a spring shut up, a fountain sealed.
> Thy plants are an orchard of pomegranates, with pleasant fruits; camphire, with spikenard,
> Spikenard and saffron; calamus and cinnamon, with all trees of frankincense; myrrh and aloes, with all the chief spices:
> A fountain of gardens, a well of living waters, and streams from Lebanon.

From the earliest times love in the garden has been associated with music-making. Many mediaeval pictures, illuminations, and tapestries depict both activities being pursued in garden settings. In the illustration to *The Romance of the Rose* (from which we have already quoted) the principal occupation of the inhabitants of the comfortably walled-in garden is love-making to the accompaniment of lyre or lute and the splash of fountains.

In other pictures, of many ages, *al fresco* meals add to the enjoyment. In Renaissance times, the banqueting house became a feature of gardens, reaching England in Tudor times. These charming buildings were essentially of the garden and not the house. The banquets held within them were not heavy meals such as we now associate with the word, but entertainments with music and dancing and masques at which light refreshments were served: at them, love no doubt played its part, as it did in the gardens of Kin-sai (Hang-chau), the capital of Kublai Khan, described by Marco Polo. These accord well with Kin-sai's standing as the Celestial City, with its 'pre-eminence to all others in the world, in point of grandeur and beauty, as well from its abundant delights, which might lead an inhabitant to image himself in paradise'. Marco describes herbs and fruits, particularly the peaches, apricots, and pears of great size, and writes of pleasure gardens which were essentially places of assignation:

> The main street of the city is paved with stone and brick to the width of ten paces on each side, the intermediate part being filled up with small gravel, and provided with arched drains for carrying off the rainwater. On this gravel carriages continually pass and repass. They are of long shape, covered at top, have curtains and cushions of silk, and are capable of holding six persons. Both men and women who feel disposed to take their pleasures are in the daily practice of hiring them for that purpose, and accordingly at every hour you may see vast numbers of them driven along the middle part of the street. Some of them proceed to visit certain gardens where the company are introduced, by those who have the management of the place, to shady recesses contrived by the gardeners for that purpose. Here the men indulge themselves all day in the society of their women, returning home, when it becomes late, in the manner they came.

The more romantic and poetic delights of love in a garden are suggested by John Lyly in the pages of his *Euphues*:

One of the Ladies who delighted much in mirth, seeing Philautus behold Camilla so stedfastly, saide unto him; Gentleman, what floure like you best in all this border; heare be faire Roses, sweete Violets, fragrant primroses, heere will be Jilly-floures, Carnations, sops in wine, Sweet Johns, and what may either please you for sight, or delight you with savour: loth we are you should have a Posie of all, yet willing to give you one as you shal lyke best.

Philautus omitting no opportunities, that might either manifest his affection, or commend his wit, answered her thus:

Lady, of so many sweet floures to chuse the best, it is harde, seeing they be all so good. If I shoulde preferre the fairest before the sweetest, you would happely imagine that I were either stopped in the nose, or wanton in the eyes; if the sweetnesse before the beautie, then would you gesse me either to lyve with savours, or to have no judgement in colours; but to tell my minde (upon correction be it spoken), of all flowers, I love a faire woman.

In deede, quoth Flavia (for so was she named) faire women are set thicke, but they come up thinne; and when they begin to budde, they are gathered as though they wer blowne. Of such men as you are, Gentlemen, who thinke greene grasse will never be drye Hay, but when ye flower of their youth (being slipped too young) shall fade before they be olde, then I dare saye, you would change your faire flower for a weede and the woman you loved then, for the worst violet you refuse now.

There is a good documentary description of a mediaeval garden in that romantic poem, *The Kingis Quair*, written by King James I of Scotland in 1423 and 1424, when he was a prisoner in England and about the time of his marriage to Lady Jane Beaufort, who was clearly the heroine of the poem, the beautiful lady whom the royal prisoner sees walking in the garden below the window of his chamber:

> Now was there maid fast by the touris wall
>   A gardyn faire, and in the corneris set
> Ane herbere grene, with wandis long and small
>   Railit about, and so with treis set
>   Was all the place, and hawthorn hegis knet,
> That lyf was not walkyng there forbye,
> That myght within scarce ony wight aspye.

So thick the beuis and the leves grene
    Beschadit all the allyes that there were,
And myddis every herbere mycht be sene
    The scharpe grene suete jenepere,
    Growing so fair with branchis here and there,
That, as it semyt to a lyf without,
The bewis spred the herbere all about.

And on the smale grene twistis sat
    The lytil suete nyghtingale, and song
So loud and clere, the ympnis consecrat
    Of luvis use, now soft now lowd among,
    That all the gardynis and the wallis rong
Ryght of thaire song, and on the copill next
Of thaire suete armony, and lo the text. . . .

And therewith kest I doun myn eye ageyne,
    Quhare as I saw walkyng under the tour,
Full secretely, new cumyn hir to pleyne,
    The fairest or the freschest younge floure
    That ever I sawe, methought, before that houre,
For quhich sodayne abate, anon astert
The blude of all my body to my hert.

Having described the violent effect of the vision of this lady upon his 'wittis', his 'eyen', and his 'hert', the royal author asks:

Ah! suete, are ye a warldly creature,
Or hevinly thing in likeness of nature?

Or are ye god Cupidis owin princesse?
    And cumyn are to louse me out of band,
Or are ye veray Nature the goddesse,
    That have depayntit with your hevinly hand
This gardyn full of flouris, as they stand?

In George Thorneley's seventeenth-century translation of *Daphnis and Chloe* there is a pleasant description of the garden in which the God of Love himself was to be found sporting. The aged Philetas addresses Daphnis and Chloe as follows:

I have a Garden which my own hands and labour planted; and . . . to dresse and trim it has been my care and entertainment; what flowers, or fruits the season of the year teems, there they are at every season. In the spring there are Roses, and Lillies, the Hyacinths, and both the forms of Violets. In the Summer, Poppies, Pears, and all sorts of Apples. And now in the Autumne Vines, and Figtrees, Pomegranats, Oranges, Limons, and the green Myrtles. Into this Garden, flocks of birds come every morning; some to feed, some to sing. For it is thick, opacous, and shady; and watered all by three fountains; and if you took the Wall away, you would think you saw a Wood.

As I went in there yesterday about noon, a boy appear'd in the Pomegranate and Myrtle grove, with Myrtles and Pomegranats in his hand; white as milk, and shining with the glance of fire; clean and bright, as if he had newly wash't himself in all the three transparent Fountains. Naked he was, alone he was; he play'd and wanton'd it about, and cull'd and pull'd as if it had been his own Garden. Therefore I ran at him as fast as I could, thinking to get him in my clutches. For indeed, I was afraid, lest, by that wanton, untoward, malapert ramping, and hoytie-toitie which he kept in the grove; he would at length break my Pomegranats, and my Myrtles. But he, with a soft and easie sleight, as he listed, gave me the slip, sometimes running under the Roses, sometimes hiding himself in the Poppies, like a cunning hudling chick of a Partridge. . . .

When Philetas had quite failed to catch the intruder he asked him who he was, whereupon the boy, having turned himself into an old man, told Philetas that he came to the garden every day to bathe in the fountains, and the reason why the flowers flourished so well was because 'they are water'd with my wash'.

This said, the sweet boy sprung into the myrtle grove, and like a Nightingale, from bough to bough, under the green leaves, skipt to the top, and highest story of the Myrtles. Then I saw his wings hanging at his shoulders; and at his back, between his wings, a little bow with two Darts; and, since that moment, never saw him any more.

It was the Elizabethan lyric poets who first raised floral analogy to the heights of amatory expression. In such a poem as the following, by Henry

Constable, brief though it is, the analogy extends beyond the obvious beauties of appearance to colour, scent, and the effects of both sun and rain:

> My Ladie's presence makes the Roses red,
>> Because to see her lips they blush for shame.
>> The Lyllie's leaves (for envie) pale became,
> And her white hands in them this envie bred.
> The Marigold the leaves abroad doth spred,
>> Because the sunne's and her power is the same.
>> The Violet of purple cullour came,
> Di'd in the blood she made my hart to shed.
> In brief, all flowers from her their vertue take;
>> From her sweet breath their sweet smels do proceede;
> The living heate which her eyebeames doth make
>> Warmeth the ground and quickeneth the seede.
>>> The rain, wherewith shee watereth the flowers,
>>> Falls from mine eyes, which she dissolves in showers.

The element of scent was evidently of great importance to the Elizabethans, and nobody developed this theme in the love lyric as elaborately and persuasively as Edmund Spenser in this sonnet:

> Comming to kisse her lyps (such grace I found)
>> Me seemd I smelt a gardin of sweet flowres,
> That dainty odours from them threw around
>> For damzels fit to decke their lovers' bowres.
> Her lips did smell lyke unto Gillyflowers,
>> Her ruddy cheekes like unto Roses red,
> Her snowy browes lyke budded Bellamoures,
>> Her lovely eyes lyke Pincks but newly spred;
> Her goodly bosome like a Strawberry bed,
>> Her neck lyke to a bounch of Cullambynes,
> Her brest lyke lillyes ere theyr leaves be shed,
>> Her nipples lyke yong blossomed Jessemynes.
>>> Such fragrant flowres doe give most odorous smell;
>>> But her sweet odour did them all excell.

One could pursue for hours—indeed for weeks and months—the floral similes of the Elizabethans—similes that curiously reflect in literary form the manifold floral conceits and patterns in the embroideries so elaborately worked for bed-hangings, valances, and table-cloths. A less obvious and to our purpose rather more revealing study is of the verses which actually place the loved one in a garden setting or compare her with the design of the garden. The following lines from a sonnet by Thomas Watson, published in *The Tears of Fancie* in 1593, give a curiously vivid impression of the Elizabethan garden scene:

> I saw the object of my pining thought
>   Within a garden of sweete nature's placing,
> Wherein an arbour, artificiall wrought,
>   By workeman's wondrous skill the garden gracing,
> Did boast his glorie, glorie farre renowned,
>   For in his shadie boughs my Mistres slept,
> And, with a garland of his branches crowned,
>   Her daintie forehead from the sunne ykept.

There is a vivid evocation of the garden scene, too, in Nicholas Breton's charming address to the garden birds:

> Sweet birds, that sit and sing amid the shadie valleys,
> And see how sweetly Phillis walks amid her garden alleys,
> Go round about her bower, and sing as ye are bidden:
> To her is only knowne his faith that from the world is hidden.
> And she among you all that hath the sweetest voice,
> Go chirpe of him that never told, yet never chang'd, his choice.

Perhaps the loveliest of all Elizabethan evocations of love in a garden is by an otherwise almost unknown poet, Bartholomew Griffin, who published a collection of sonnets in 1596 entitled *Fidessa, More Chaste than Kinde*:

> Faire is my love that feedes among the Lillies,
>   The Lillies growing in that pleasant garden
> Where Cupid's mount that welbeloved hill is,
>   And where that little god himselfe is warden.
> See where my Love sits in the beds of spices,
>   Beset all round with Camphere, Myrrhe and Roses,
> And interlac'd with curious devices,

Which her, from all the world apart, incloses.
There doth she tune her Lute for her delight,
And with sweet musick makes the ground to move,
Whilst I, poore I, doe sit in heavie plight,
Wayling alone my unrespected love,
Not daring rush into so rare a place,
That gives to her, and she to it, a grace.

In most of these Elizabethan lyrics, one observes, the object of adoration is static, set in an arbour, enshrined in a bower, or sitting among the lilies. Is it perhaps a sign of the times—the increased horticultural activity of the Stuart ladies who were so copiously instructed by Markham, Hill, and other gardening journalists—that the loved ones seem to be much more on the move in the amatory garden verse of the mid-seventeenth century? One of the finest, but still least-known, examples is that by Nathaniel Hookes, published in 1653:

And now what Monarch would not Gard'ner be,
My faire Amanda's stately gate to see;
How her feet tempt! how soft and light she treads,
Fearing to wake the flowers from their beds!
Yet from their sweet green pillowes ev'ry where,
They start and gaze about to see my Faire;
Look at yon flower yonder, how it growes
Sensibly! how it opes its leaves and blowes,
Puts its best Easter clothes on, neat and gay!
Amanda's presence makes it holy-day:
Look how on tip-toe that faire lilie stands
To look on thee, and court thy whiter hands
To gather it! I saw in yonder croud
The Tulip-bed, of which Dame-Flora's proud,
A short dwarfe flower did enlarge its stalk,
And shoot an inch to see Amanda walk; ...
The gravell'd walkes, tho ev'n as a die,
Lest some loose pebble should offensive lie,
Quilt themselves o're with downie moss for thee;
The walls are hang'd with blossom'd tapestrie
To hide their nakednesse when look'd upon;
The maiden fig tree puts Eve's apron on;

The broad-leav'd Sycomore, and ev'ry tree
Shakes like the trembling Aspe, and bends to thee,
And each leaf proudly strives with fresher aire,
To fan the curlèd tresses of thy hair;
Nay, and the Bee too, with his wealthie thigh,
Mistakes his hive, and to thy lips doth flie;
Willing to treasure up his honey there,
Where honey-combs so sweet and plenty are:
Look how that pretty modest Columbine
Hangs down its head to view those feet of thine!
See the fond motion of the Strawberrie,
Creeping on th'earth, to go along with thee!
The lovely violet makes after too,
Unwilling yet, my Dear, to part with you;
The knot-grasse and the dazies catch thy toes
To catch my faire ones feet before she goes;
All court and wish me lay Amanda down,
And give my Dear a new green flower'd gown.
Come let me kisse thee falling, kisse at rise,
Thou in the Garden, I in Paradise.

What might be called 'seed catalogue' verses became popular about this time—lines in which a series of flowers were invoked to testify to the beloved's charms. An example is a poem included by an obscure author, John Reynolds, in his appropriately entitled miscellany, *The Flower of Fidelitie*, published in 1650:

Say, Crimson-Rose, and dainty Daffadil,
    With Violet blew;
Since you have seen the beauty of my Saint,
    And eke her view,
Did not her sight (fair sight) you lovely fill
    With sweet delight
Of Goddesse grace and Angel's sacred taint
    In fine most bright?

Say, golden Prim-rose, sanguine Couslip faire,
    With Pinck most fine,
Since you beheld the Visage of my Dear,
    And Eyes divine,

Did not her globy Front, and glistering Hair,
    With Cheeks most sweet,
So gloriously like Damask flowers appear,
    The gods to greet?

Say, snow-white Lily, speckled Gilly-flower,
    With Daisie gay,
Since you have viewed the Queen of my desire
    In brave array,
Did not her Ivory Paps, fair Venus' Bower,
    With heavenly glee
Of Juno's grace, conjure you to require
    Her face to see?

Say Rose, say Daffadil, and Violet blew,
    With Primerose faire,
Since you have seen my Nymph's sweet dainty-face
    And gesture rare,
Did not, bright Couslip, bloomy Pinck, her view
    White Lilly, shine,
Ah, Gilly-flowers, and Daisie, with a grace
    Like Stars divine?

There is an Elizabethan prodigality of floral references in this poem, but in general the poets of the seventeenth century tended to concentrate their amatory images upon the rose. Possibly because poets were becoming increasingly urban in their outlook, and their imagery was becoming increasingly artificial or metaphysical, the rose became the conventional—because the most obvious—symbol of beauty and messenger of love.

Sweet serene skye-like Flower,
Haste to adorn her Bower,
    From thy long clowdy bed
    Shoot forth thy damaske head.

New-startled blush of *Flora*!
The griefe of pale *Aurora*,
    Who will contest no more,
    Haste, haste to strowe her floore.

Vermilion Ball that's given
From lip to lip in Heaven,
    Love's couch's cover-led,
    Haste, haste to make her bed.

Dear Offspring of pleas'd *Venus*
And Jollie, plumpe *Silenus*,
    Haste, haste to decke the Haire
    Of th' only, sweetly Faire.

See! Rosie is her Bower,
Her floore is all this Flower,
    Her Bed a Rosie nest
    By a Bed of Roses prest.

But early as she dresses,
Why fly you her bright Tresses?
    Ah! I have found I feare;
    Because her Cheekes are neere.

So Richard Lovelace addressed his Lucasta in 1649. Of all poems about love and the rose, however, surely the most perfectly turned and eloquent is Edmund Waller's, published in 1645:

Go, lovely Rose,
Tell her that wasts her time and me,
    That now she knows,
When I resemble her to thee,
How sweet and fair she seems to be.

    Tell her that's young,
And shuns to have her graces spy'd
    That hadst thou sprung
In desarts, where no men abide,
Thou must have uncommended dy'd.

    Small is the worth
Of beauty from the light retir'd:
    Bid her come forth,
Suffer her self to be desir'd,
And not blush so to be admir'd.

> Then die, that she
> The common fate of all things rare
> May read in thee;
> How small a part of time they share
> That are so wondrous sweet and fair.

During the eighteenth century garden verse, if we may thus describe it, became increasingly artificial, as is shown by some lyrics we have quoted earlier in this book. The eighteenth century was the great period of didactic verse in English literature, and a period when science was still a poetic subject. In the Garden of Love should we forget the loves of the plants themselves? Dr Erasmus Darwin (no stranger to the tender passion) wrote many pages of rhyme—at times even poetry—tuning his oaten reed to sing the

> Gay hopes, and amorous sorrows of the mead—
> From giant oaks, that wave their branches dark,
> To the dwarf moss that clings upon their bark
> What beaux and beauties crowd the gaudy groves
> And woo and win their vegetable loves.

The story of the vegetable loves proceeds:

> First the tall Canna lifts his curled brow
> Erect to heaven, and plights his nuptial vow;
> The virtuous pair, in milder regions born,
> Dread the rude blast of autumn's icy morn;
> Round the chill fair he holds his crimson vest,
> And clasps the timorous beauty to his breast. . . .

> Sweet blooms Genista in the myrtle shade,
> And ten fond brothers woo the haughty maid.
> Two knights before thy fragrant altar bend,
> Adored Melissa! and two squires attend.—
> Meadia's soft chains five suppliant beaux confess,
> And hand in hand the laughing belle address;
> Alike to all she bows with wanton air,
> Rolls her dark eye, and waves her golden hair.
> Woo'd with long care, Curcuma cold and shy
> Meets her fond husband with averted eye:
> Four beardless youths the obdurate beauty move
> With soft attentions of Platonic love.

With vain desires the pensive Alcea burns,
And, like said Eloisa, loves and mourns.
The freckled Iris owns a fiercer flame,
And three unjealous husbands wed the dame.
Cupressus dark disdains his dusky bride,
One dome contains them, but two beds divide.
The proud Osyris flies his angry fair,
Two houses hold the fashionable pair.
With strange deformity Plantago treads,
A monster birth! and lifts his hundred heads
Yet with soft love a gentle belle he charms
And clasps the beauty in his hundred arms.
So hapless Desdemona, fair and young,
Won by Othello's captivating tongue,
Sigh'd o'er each strange and piteous tale, distress'd,
And sunk enamour'd on his sooty breast. . . .
When o'er the cultured lawns and dreary wastes
Retiring autumn flings her howling blasts,
Bends in the tumultuous waves the struggling woods,
And showers their leafy honours on the floods,
In withering heaps collects the flowery spoil,
And each chill insect sinks beneath the soil.
Quick flies fair Tulipa the loud alarms;
And folds her infant closer in her arms;
In some lone cave, secure pavilion, lies,
And waits the courtship of serener skies.—
So, six cold moons, the dormouse charm'd to rest.
Indulgent sleep! beneath thy eider breast,
In fields of fancy climbs the kernel'd groves,
Or shares the golden harvests with his loves.—
Then bright from earth, amid the troubled sky
Ascends fair Colchica with radiant eye,
Warms the cold bosom of the hoary year,
And lights with beauty's blaze the dusky sphere.
Three blushing maids, the intrepid nymph attend.
And six gay youths, enamour'd train! defend.
So shines with silver guards the Georgian star,
And drives on night's blue arch his glittering car;
Hangs o'er the billowy clouds his lucid form,
Wades through the mist, and dances in the storm.

The key to this delightful account of the vegetable loves is found in the first of the author's footnotes—which rival the poem in their length: 'Linneus, the celebrated Swedish naturalist, has demonstrated, that all flowers contain families of males or females, or both; and on their marriages has constructed his invaluable system of Botany'.

Another, and less solemn, element in the eighteenth century Garden of Love was the garden party, whether it was the gathering of gay spirits in the English pleasure gardens of Ranelagh or Vauxhall, or the *fêtes galantes* of the French nobility. The scene of the 'gallant conversations' in England was vividly conjured up by Smollett in *Humphrey Clinker* in 1771:

> Image to yourself, my dear Letty, a spacious garden, part laid out in delightful walks, bounded with high hedges and trees, and paved with gravel; part exhibiting a wonderful assemblage of the most picturesque and striking objects, pavilions, lodges, groves, grottoes, lawns, temples, and cascades; porticoes, colonades, and rotundos; adorned with pillars, statues, and painting; the whole illuminated with an infinite number of lamps, disposed in different figures of suns, stars, and constellations; the place crowded with the gayest company, ranging through those blissful shades, or supping in different lodges on cold collations, enlivened with mirth, freedom, and good humour, and animated by an excellent band of music. Among the vocal performers I had the happiness to hear the celebrated Mrs ——, whose voice was loud and so shrill that it made my head ache through excess of pleasure.

Vauxhall and Ranelagh, however, were public places, and the essence of a Garden of Love is that it should provide privacy. There is certainly an appropriate air of privacy about the riverside garden described in 1749 by John Cleland in his *Memoirs of a Woman of Pleasure*, a novel which has subsequently become notorious under the name of its heroine, Fanny Hill:

> Everything being settled, and it being a fine summer day, but rather of the warmest, we set out after dinner, and got to our rendez-vous about four in the afternoon; where, landing at the foot of a neat, joyous pavilion, Emily and I were ushered by our squires, and

there drank tea with a cheerfulness and gaiety to which the beauty of the prospect, the serenity of the weather, and the tender politeness of our sprightly gallants naturally led us.

After tea, and taking a turn in the garden, my particular, who was the master of the house, and had in no sense schem'd this party of pleasure for a dry one, propos'd to us, with that frankness which his familiarity at Mrs Cole's entitled him to, as the weather was excessively hot, to bathe together, under a commodious shelter that he had prepared expressly for that purpose, in a creek of the river, with which a side door of the pavilion immediately communicated, and where we might be sure of having our diversion out, safe from interruption, and with the utmost privacy.

Emily, who never refused anything, and I, who ever delighted in bathing, and had no exception to the person who proposed it, or to those pleasures it was easy to guess it implied, took care, on this occasion, not to forget our training at Mrs Cole's, and agreed to it with as good a grace as we could. Upon which, without loss of time, we returned instantly to the pavilion, one door of which open'd into a tent, pitch'd before it, that with its marquise, formed a pleasing defense against the sun, or the weather, and was besides as private as we could wish. The lining of it, emboss'd cloth, represented a wild, forest-foliage, from the top, down to the sides, which, in the same stuff, were figur'd with fluted pilasters, with their spaces between fill'd with flower-vases, the whole having a gay effect upon the eye, wherever you turn'd it.

Then it reached sufficiently into the water, yet contained convenient benches round it, on the dry ground, either to keep our clothes, or . . . or . . . in short for more uses than resting upon. There was a side-table too, loaded with sweetmeats, jellies, and other eatables, and bottles of wine and cordials, by way of occasional relief from any rawness, or chill of the water, or from any faintness from whatever cause; and in fact, my gallant, who understood *chère entière* perfectly, and who, for taste (even if you would not approve this specimen of it) might have been comptroller of pleasures to a Roman emperor, had left no requisite towards convenience or luxury unprovided.

They ordered these things not so very differently in France, as is evident from the *fêtes galantes* depicted so enchantingly in the paintings of Watteau, Lancret, Pater and Fragonard.

It is odd that the French pictorial conventions of the *fête galante* hardly seemed to cross the English Channel. That gallantry thrived in England in the Augustan Age is made evident in the plays of Congreve and Farquhar and in a thousand lyrics by minor poets. When it came to painting, however, it would seem that English patrons were reluctant to invest in frivolities. If a patron wanted an elegant group in a garden setting he wasn't interested in seeing his friends dressed up, as Watteau's were, like Harlequin and Columbine, or, as Fragonard's were, like nymphs and shepherds. He liked to get for his money a straightforward conversation piece of himself and his wife and his children—to say nothing of a few aunts, the pug dog, and a favourite hunter.

Quite a number of English conversation pieces of the mid-eighteenth century have garden settings, but the romantic element is presented with great reserve. The inspiration is not Gallantry but Matrimony. There is an interesting example of this in the conversation piece by Francis Hayman which is believed to portray George Rogers and his young wife, Margaret Tyers, daughter of Jonathan Tyers, the proprietor of Vauxhall Gardens.

It is evident that this exquisite painting is essentially a 'garden picture'. The stone urn before which the couple are posed might well have been one of the garden ornaments of Vauxhall (for which Hayman was commissioned by his friend Tyers to paint a series of murals). How does one account for the somewhat incongruous suggestion of a cornfield in the background of what is otherwise a formal park-like setting?

The answer may be found by comparing this picture with Gainsborough's famous painting of Mr and Mrs Robert Andrews, now in the National Gallery in London. There, too, the young couple are posed against the background of a cornfield. Clearly both pictures were painted as marriage portraits, and the cornfield is a symbolic element, the ripe ears signifying fertility.

Much more frivolous was the inspiration of the amatory garden scenes painted in France and Italy about the same time by Fragonard. To him we owe some of the most vivid evocations of the gardens of the Villa d'Este, and the lovely series of four paintings of 'The Loves of the Shepherds', now in the Frick Collection in New York, which were

Francis Hayman, RA. Margaret Tyers and her husband. c. 1745.
Mr and Mrs Paul Mellon.

Jean Honoré Fragonard. Love Letters. 1771.
New York, The Frick Collection.

originally commissioned by the Comtesse du Barry in 1771 for the Château of Louveciennes, but were rejected, possibly because Louis XV may have recognized his own portrait in the Lover. These pictures breathe the very air and spirit of the French formal garden of the time.

But the eighteenth century came to an end, and the Romantic Movement swept away the pretty artificial romances of the Court of Marie Antoinette. Lovers now sought in the garden for depth of emotion, for sincerity and sensibility, for intimations of immortality.

> We paced about the garden happily,
> And all things paid us homage: the green boughs
> In their deep shadows folded us; soft vows,
> Of balmy gentleness, seemed audibly
> From every night breeze on our ears to die;
> And, in the beauty of their dim repose,
> The flowers appeared to dream of us, and close
> Their shut eyes closer for felicity!
> And then came higher sympathies: the stars
> Began their lofty coming: and the moon
> Forth issued from the throbbing blue of heaven—
> That, for our loves the Universe seemed given:
> In our hearts all things, and our hearts in theirs,
> Suffused in beatific interswoon!

So wrote Thomas Wade in *The Monthly Depository* of December 1837, the year of Queen Victoria's accession. It is remarkable how instantaneously the peculiar solemnity and religiosity that we associate with the Victorian age manifested itself in Mr Wade's 'beatific interswoon'.

In the same year the spirit of the Victorian garden expressed itself, less ponderously but more durably, in the prose of an apprentice novelist, Charles Dickens:

> 'I have forgotten my flowers,' said the spinster aunt.
> 'Water them now,' said Mr Tupman, in accents of persuasion.
> 'You will take cold in the evening air,' urged the spinster aunt, affectionately.
> 'No, no,' said Mr Tupman, rising; 'it will do me good. Let me accompany you.'

The lady paused to adjust the sling in which the left arm of the youth was placed, and taking his right arm led him to the garden.

There was a bower at the further end, with honeysuckle, jessamine, and creeping plants—one of those sweet retreats which humane men erect for the accommodation of spiders.

The spinster aunt took up a large watering-pot which lay in one corner, and was about to leave the arbour. Mr Tupman detained her, and drew her to a seat beside him.

'Miss Wardle!' said he.

The spinster aunt trembled, till some pebbles which had accidentally found their way into the large watering-pot shook like an infant's rattle.

'Miss Wardle,' said Mr Tupman, 'you are an angel.'

'Mr Tupman!' exclaimed Rachael, blushing as red as the watering-pot itself.

'Nay,' said the eloquent Pickwickian—'I know it but too well.'

'All women are angels, they say,' murmured the lady, playfully.

'Then what can *you* be; or to what, without presumption, can I compare you?' replied Mr Tupman. 'Where was the woman ever seen, who resembled you? Where else could I hope to find so rare a combination of excellence and beauty? Where else could I seek to —Oh!' Here Mr Tupman paused, and pressed the hand which clasped the handle of the happy watering-pot.

The watering-pot was the only consolation of an enamoured gardener of about the same period, but of markedly lower social status. His plaint was expressed in an anonymous street ballad:

> I'm a broken-hearted Gardener, and don't know what to do,
> My love she is inconstant, and a fickle jade, too,
> One smile from her lips will never be forgot,
> It refreshes, like a shower from a watering pot.

> CHORUS: Oh, Oh! she's a fickle wild rose,
>   A damask, a cabbage, a young China Rose.

> She's my myrtle, my geranium,
> My Sun flower, my sweet marjorum.
> My honey suckle, my tulip, my violet,
> My holy hock, my dahlia, my mignonette.

A BROKEN-HEARTED GARDENER

We grew up together like two apple trees,
And clung to each other like double sweet peas,
Now they're going to trim her, and plant her in a pot,
And I'm left to wither, neglected and forgot.

She's my snow drop, my ranunculus,
My hyacinth, my gilliflower, my polyanthus,
My heart's ease, my pink water lily,
My buttercup, my daisy, my daffydown dilly.

I'm like a scarlet runner that has lost its stick,
Or a cherry that's left for the dickey to pick,
Like a waterpot I weep, like a paviour I sigh,
Like a mushroom I'll wither, like a cucumber, die.

I'm like a humble bee that doesn't know where to settle,
And she's a dandelion, and a stinging nettle,
My heart's like a beet root choked with chickweed,
And my head's like a pumpkin running to seed.

I'm a great mind to make myself a felo-de-se,
And finish all my woes on the branch of a tree:
But I won't, for I know at my kicking you'd roar,
And honour my death with a double encore.

A healthier if more ruthless view of love is taken in an American ballad of the same vintage which is one of the few poems to put on the poetic map that unprepossessing plant, the cactus:

Haughty lady, discard that look
    So like a cactus the wind has weathered;
With patience, time, and a little hook
    Even the green fruit may be gathered.

Observe that remnant of a tree
    Which a green Providence has fathered;
Time has no gift of sympathy
    And winter's favors leave all withered.

Observe your cactus of the plains,
    Proud of its drouth, so long unwatered.
But what avail the arrogant rains
    When, for its sweets, the trunk is shattered.

Haughty lady, discard that look
    So like a cactus the wind has weathered;
With patience, time, and a little hook
    Even the green fruit may be gathered.

But this is not the characteristic attitude of the Victorian age. Sensibility was the thing, and at its highest level it found a voice in the sonnets of Elizabeth Barrett Browning:

Beloved, thou has brought me many flowers
    Plucked in the garden, all the summer through
    And winter, and it seemed as if they grew
In this close room, nor missed the sun and showers.
So, in the like name of that love of ours,
    Take back these thoughts which here unfolded too,
    And which on warm and cold days I withdrew
From my heart's ground. Indeed, those beds and bowers
    Be overgrown with bitter weeds and rue,
And wait thy weeding; yet here's eglantine,
    Here's ivy!—take them, as I used to do
Thy flowers, and keep them where they shall not pine.
    Instruct thine eyes to keep their colours true,
And tell thy soul their roots are left in mine.

At a rather lower level of poetic diction, but with an even more heart-rending display of the tears and tribulations of the Victorian spirit, Alexander Smith—a virtually forgotten poet, alas!—addressed his discarded loved one in 1853, from various recumbent, kneeling, or erect postures in the garden:

The broken moon lay in the autumn sky,
    And I lay at thy feet;
You bent over me; in the silence I
    Could hear my wild heart beat ...

You kissed me then, I worshipped at thy feet
    Upon the shadowy sod.
Oh, fool, I loved thee! loved thee, lovely cheat!
    Better than Fame or God...

Before your window, as before a shrine,
    I've knelt 'mong dew-soaked flowers,
While distant music-bells, with voices fine,
    Measured the midnight hours.

There came a fearful moment: I was pale,
    You wept, and never spoke,
But clung around me as the woodbine frail
    Clings, pleading, round an oak.

Upon my wrong I steadied up my soul,
    And flung thee from myself;
I spurned thy love as 't were a rich man's dole,—
    It was my only wealth...

Too late, thy fatal beauty and thy tears,
    Thy vows, thy passionate breath;
I'll meet thee not in Life, nor in the spheres
    Made visible by Death.

The Victorians were, as is evident from so many of the story-paintings and problem pictures of the time, deeply 'mixed-up'—to use a modern phrase—in their personal relationships. They were often deeply troubled by emotional and moral complexities which are—if one ventures to risk the parallel—faithfully reflected in the complex carpet bedding, the meandering gravel paths, the darkling shrubberies, and the heady excursions into the exotic—the deodars, the monkey puzzles—of the Victorian garden. This parallel is relentlessly pursued by Arthur William Edgar O'Shaughnessy, a poet of the 'seventies:

    I made another garden, yea
        For my new love;
    I left the dead rose where it lay
        And set the new above.

Why did my Summer not begin?
　　Why did my heart not haste?
My old love came and walk'd therein
　　And laid the garden waste.

She enter'd with her weary smile,
　　Just as of old;
She look'd around a little while
　　And shiver'd at the cold:
Her passing touch was death to all,
　　Her passing look a blight;
She made the white rose-petals fall,
　　And turn'd the red rose white.

Her pale robe clinging to the grass
　　Seem'd like a snake
That bit the grass and ground, alas!
　　And a sad trail did make.
She went up slowly to the gate,
　　And then, just as of yore,
She turn'd back at the last to wait
　　And say farewell once more.

About the time these bitter lines were written the Rev Francis
Kilvert, a curate in the remote parish of Clyro in Radnorshire, Wales, had
fallen in love. On 13 September 1871, he recorded in his diary:

> An ever memorable day in my life. I went to the Vicarage at
> 10 o'clock and had a long talk . . . about my attachment to Daisy. . . .
> The whole family at home came into the drawing room to see me
> and I was wondering how I could get Mr Thomas away for a private
> talk, when he said suddenly, 'Come out into the garden.' Daisy came
> into the room. I thought she coloured and looked conscious. Then
> we went out into the garden, her father and I.
> I said, 'You will be very much surprised but I hope not displeased
> at what I am going to say to you.' 'What is it?' he said eagerly, 'have
> you got the living of Glasbury?' 'No, something much nearer to you
> than that.' 'What is it?' I was silent a minute. I was frightfully
> nervous.

'I-am-attached-to-one-of-your-daughters,' I said. Just as I made this avowal we came suddenly round the corner upon a gardener cutting a hedge. I feared he had heard my confession, but I was much relieved by being assured that he was deaf. Mr Thomas said I had done quite right in coming to him, though he seemed a good deal taken aback.

He said also a great many complimentary things about 'my honourable high-minded conduct', asked what my prospects were and shook his head over them. He could not allow an engagement under the circumstances, he said, and I must not destroy his daughter's peace of mind by speaking to her or showing her in any way that I was attached to her ... 'Long engagements are dreadful things'. . . .

Well, I thought to myself, whatever I suffer she shall not suffer if I can help it. We had been walking along the path between the house and the garden and down the middle garden walk. The place is inextricably entwined in my remembrance with the conversation and the circumstances. I felt deeply humiliated, low in spirit and sick at heart. . . . What has happened only makes me long for her more and cling more closely to her. . . .

I went back across the brook with sorrowful heart. . . . At Cae Mawr I found my sisters and Tom Williams playing croquet and just driven into the verandah by the rain. The afternoon had been grey, dull and dismal with an E. dark wind. Everything seemed gloomy and cold and the evening was irksome. I could not feel able to join in the Bezique at Cae Mawr.

How often in history—and not only in Victorian times—has a suitor been invited to 'take a turn in the garden' with a prospective father-in-law! But this book is concerned with delights, not with humiliation, sickness at heart, and the 'E. dark wind'. Let us leave the Garden of Love to the verbal music of what surely remains, despite its familiarity, despite burlesque, one of the most moving garden poems of all time.

> Come into the garden, Maud,
>   For the black bat, night, has flown,
> Come into the garden, Maud,
>   I am here at the gate alone;
> And the woodbine spices are wafted abroad,
>   And the musk of the rose is blown. . . .

THE GARDEN OF LOVE

All night have the roses heard
　　The flute, violin, bassoon;
All night has the casement jessamine stirr'd
　　To the dancers dancing in tune;
Till a silence fell with a waking bird,
　　And a hush with the setting moon.

I said to the lily, 'There is but one
　　With whom she has heart to be gay.
When will the dancers leave her alone?
　　She is weary of dance and play.'
Now half to the setting moon are gone,
　　And half to the rising day;
Low on the sand and loud on the stone
　　The last wheel echoes away.

I said to the rose, 'The brief night goes
　　In babble and revel and wine.
O young lord-lover, what sighs are those,
　　For one that will never be thine?
But mine, mine' so I sware to the rose,
　　'For ever and ever, mine.' . . .

Queen rose of the rosebud garden of girls,
　　Come hither, the dances are done,
In gloss of satin and glimmer of pearls,
　　Queen lily and rose in one;
Shine out, little head, sunning over with curls,
　　To the flowers, and be their sun.

There has fallen a splendid tear
　　From the passion-flower at the gate
She is coming, my dove, my dear;
　　She is coming, my life, my fate;
The red rose cries, 'She is near, she is near';
　　And the white rose weeps, 'She is late';
The larkspur listens, 'I hear, I hear';
　　And the lily whispers, 'I wait.'

Arthur Hughes. The Tryst. c. 1850-5. *London, Tate Gallery.*

Maurice Denis. Paradise. 1912.

1s. *Paris, Musée d'Art Moderne.*

Wall painting in the Hof burg, Imperial Palace, Innsbruck, depicting three children of Maria Theresa, who died in childhood, arriving in Paradise. c.1770.
Photograph by Gerti Deutsch.

8

The Return to Paradise

As we wrote in the Introduction, a garden may be a re-creation on earth of the mythical garden from which man came or an anticipation of an ideal other-world to which he may ultimately pass. The gardener looks back to Paradise, or looks forward to Heaven. Both states are ideal, and, despite the vagaries of the weather, the indiscipline of weeds, and the depradations of slugs and aphides, all gardens aim at the ideal. As Marvell wrote:

> Here at the Fountains sliding foot
> Or at some Fruit-trees mossy root,
> Casting the Bodies Vest aside
> My Soul into the boughs does glide:
> There like a Bird it sits, and sings,
> Then whets, and combs its silver Wings;
> And, till prepar'd for longer flight,
> Waves in its Plumes the various Light.

One of the oddest word pictures of a Paradisal garden is to be found in that strange hotch-potch of mythology, *The Voiage and Travaile of Syr John Mandevile*. The author—himself a somewhat mythical figure—wrote about a rich man named Catalonapes living in an island belonging to Prester John, the legendary priest-king who ruled an empire in the far East. We quote from the first English edition, printed in 1568:

Catalonapes . . . had a fair castel on a hil & strong, & he made a wal all about the hil right strong & fayre, within he had a faire gardeine wherin were many trees bearing all maner of fruits that he might fynd, & he had planted therin al maner of herbs of good smel & that bare flowers, & ther wer many faire wels, . . . & he had in his gardeine al thing that might be to man solace & comfort, he had also in that gardeine maydens within the age of XV yeare, the fairest that he might find, & men children of the same age, & they were clothed with clothes of gold, & he sayd that they were aungels and he caused to be made certain hils, & enclosed them about with precious stones of Jaspy & christal & set in gold & pearls, and other maner of stones, and he had made a coundute under the earth, so that whan he wold the wals ran somtime with milke, somtime honey, & this place is called Paradise.

Sir John Mandevile went on to tell how Catalonapes used to entertain any young knight or squire who visited him by taking them into this garden, causing musical instruments to be played in a high tower, and telling his guests that what they saw and heard were the figures and voices of angels. If they fought loyally for him in battle and were slain the knights and squires would enter this earthly Paradise and live with the angels.

Allowing for minor differences in scene and period there is an uncanny resemblance between this artificial conception of Paradise Garden and the purely imaginative one created by the French artist Maurice Denis, in his picture, 'Le Paradis', painted in 1912, and now in the Musée d'Art Moderne in Paris.

Observe that both Sir John Mandevile in the sixteenth century and Maurice Denis in the twentieth visualized Paradise as being peopled by *child* angels—an obvious reflection of the idea of original innocence. Thomas Traherne, in the seventeenth century, continually touched upon this conception. Let us therefore end this book by seeking, like Peter Pan, whose statue so appropriately stands in London's Kensington Gardens, for the child's own version of Elysium, the Never-Never-Land. John Dryden, surprisingly, can set us on our way, with lines from 'The Flower and the Leaf, or The Lady in the Arbour':

> . . . I took the way
> Which through a Path, but scarcely printed, lay;
> In narrow Mazes oft it seem'd to meet,
> And look'd as lightly press'd by Fairy Feet.
> Wandring I walk'd alone, for still methought
> To some strange End so strange a Path was wrought:

THE LADY IN THE ARBOUR

At last it led me where an Arbour stood . . .
'Twas bench'd with Turf, and goodly to be seen,
The thick young Grass arose in fresher Green:
The Mound was newly made, no Sight cou'd pass
Betwixt the nice Partitions of the Grass;
The well-united Sods so closely lay;
And all arround the Shades defended it from Day.
For Sycamours with Eglantine were spread,
A Hedge about the Sides, a Covering over Head.
And so the fragrant Briar was wove between,
The Sycamour and Flow'rs were mix'd with Green,
That Nature seem'd to vary the Delight;
And satisfy'd at once the Smell and Sight.
The Master Work-man of the Bow'r was known
Through Fairy-Lands, and built for *Oberon*:
Who twining Leaves with such Proportion drew,
They rose by Measure, and by Rule they grew:
No mortal Tongue can half the Beauty tell,
For none but Hands divine could work so well,
Both Roof and Sides were like a Parlour made,
A soft Recess, and a cool Summer Shade;
The Hedge was set so thick, no Foreign Eye
The Persons plac'd within it could espy;
But all that pass'd without with Ease was seen,
As if nor Fence nor Tree was plac'd between,
'Twas border'd with a Field; and some was plain
With Grass; and some was sow'd with rising Grain,
That (now the Dew with Spangles deck'd the Ground,)
A sweeter spot of Earth was never found.
I look'd, and look'd, and still with new Delight;
Such Joy my Soul, such Pleasures fill'd my Sight:
And the fresh Eglantine exhal'd a Breath;
Whose Odours were of Pow'r to raise from Death.
Nor sullen Discontent, nor anxious Care,
Ev'n tho' brought thither, could inhabit there:
But thence they fled as from their mortal Foe;
For this sweet Place cou'd only Pleasure know . . .
My Sight, and Smell, and Hearing were employ'd,
And all three Senses in full Gust enjoy'd.
And what alone did all the rest surpass,

The sweet Possession of the Fairy Place;
Single, and conscious to my Self alone,
Of Pleasures to th'excluded World unknown.
Pleasures which no where else were to be found
And all *Elysium* in a spot of Ground.

Yes, the garden ground which we have now entered (having found the key through some mysterious agency, as Mary found the key to her Secret Garden) is the same terrain as provided the setting for *A Midsummer Night's Dream*. This is how Thomas Hood described it in his 'Plea of the Midsummer Fairies':

It was a shady and sequester'd scene,
Like those famed gardens of Boccaccio,
Planted with his own laurels evergreen,
And roses that for endless summer blow;
And there were founting springs to overflow
Their marble basins, and cool green arcades
Of tall o'erarching sycamores, to throw
Athwart the dappled path their dancing shades,
With timid coneys cropping the green blades . . .

And there were crystal pools, peopled with fish,
Argent and gold; and some of Tyrian skin,
Some crimson-barr'd;—and ever at a wish
They rose obsequious till the wave grew thin
As glass upon their backs, and then dived in,
Quenching their ardent scales in watery gloom;
Whilst others with fresh hues row'd forth to win
My changeable regard,—for so we doom
Things born of thought to vanish or to bloom.

And there were many birds of many dyes,
From tree to tree still faring to and fro,
And stately peacocks with their splendid eyes,
And gorgeous pheasants with their golden glow,
Like Iris just bedabbled in her bow,
Besides some vocalists, without a name,
That oft on fairy errands come and go,

THE IMMACULATE ROSE

With accents magical;—and all were tame,
And peckled at my hand where'er I came.

Since the Floral Queen of this garden must have been the Rose, just as Titania was its Faerie Queen—let us end with two rose poems: first an invocation to her written in the closing years of the nineteenth century by William Sharp, the author of another faerie opera, *The Immortal Hour*:

Oh, fair immaculate rose of the world, rose of my dream, my Rose!
Beyond the ultimate gates of dream I have heard thy mystical call:
It is where the rainbow of hope suspends and the river of rapture flows—
And the cool sweet dews from the wells of peace for ever fall.

And all my heart is aflame because of the rapture and peace,
And I dream, in my waking dreams and deep in the dreams of sleep,
Till the high sweet wonderful call that shall be the call of release
Shall ring in my ears as I sink from gulf to gulf and from deep to deep—

Sink deep, sink deep beyond the ultimate dreams of all desire—
Beyond the uttermost limit of all that the craving spirit knows:
Then, then, oh then I shall be as the inner flame of thy fire,
O fair immaculate rose of the world, Rose of my dream, my Rose!

Gerald Bullett expresses another facet of the same transcendent thought in these lapidary lines, 'In the Garden at Night':

Be still, my soul. Consider
    The flowers and the stars.
Among these sleeping fragrances,
    Sleep now your cares.
That which the universe
    Lacks room to enclose
Lives in the folded petals
    Of this dark rose.

Index

Entries relating to plants and trees refer only to pages on which they are discussed at length.

INDEX

INDEX